# JOAN OF ARC

## Heavenly Warrior

Tabatha Yeatts

www.sterlingpublishing.com/kids

For my father and first reader,
Harry W. Yeatts, Jr.

With deep appreciation to Benjamin Lonske, Eleanor Lonske, Quinten
Lonske, Barry Peckham, Catherine Wingfield-Yeatts, Helen D. Yeatts, Ariana
Yeatts-Lonske, Dashiell Yeatts-Lonske, Elena Yeatts-Lonske, and all the
scholars who have taken such patience and care to uncover, translate, and
share documents concerning La Pucelle.

STERLING and the distinctive Sterling logo are registered trademarks of
Sterling Publishing Co., Inc.

**Library of Congress Cataloging-in-Publication Data**
Yeatts, Tabatha.
  Joan of Arc : heavenly warrior / by Tabatha Yeatts.
     p. cm. — (Sterling biographies)
  Includes bibliographical references and index.
  ISBN 978-1-4027-5662-7 (pbk.) — ISBN 978-1-4027-6542-1 (hardcover)
  1. Joan, of Arc, Saint, 1412-1431—Juvenile literature. 2. Christian women
saints—France—Biography—Juvenile literature. 3. France—History—Charles VII,
1422-1461—Juvenile literature. I. Title.
  DC103.5.Y43 2009
  944'.026092—dc22
  [B]
                                    2008030699

10  9  8  7  6  5  4  3  2  1

Published by Sterling Publishing Co., Inc.
387 Park Avenue South, New York, NY 10016
© 2009 by Tabatha Yeatts

Distributed in Canada by Sterling Publishing
c/o Canadian Manda Group, 165 Dufferin Street
Toronto, Ontario, Canada M6K 3H6
Distributed in the United Kingdom by GMC Distribution Services
Castle Place, 166 High Street, Lewes, East Sussex, England BN7 1XU
Distributed in Australia by Capricorn Link (Australia) Pty. Ltd.
P.O. Box 704, Windsor, NSW 2756, Australia

*Printed in China*
*All rights reserved*

Sterling ISBN 978-1-4027-5662-7 (paperback)
         ISBN 978-1-4027-6542-1 (hardcover)

Image research by Larry Schwartz

For information about custom editions, special sales, premium and corporate
purchases, please contact Sterling Special Sales Department at 800-805-5489
or specialsales@sterlingpublishing.com.

# Contents

# Events in the Life of Joan of Arc

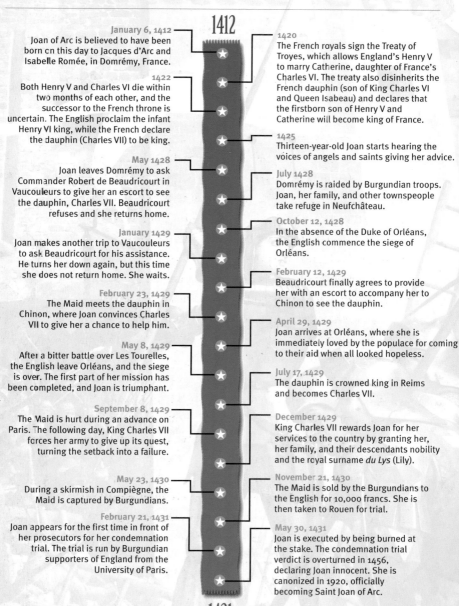

**1412**

**January 6, 1412**
Joan of Arc is believed to have been born on this day to Jacques d'Arc and Isabelle Romée, in Domrémy, France.

**1420**
The French royals sign the Treaty of Troyes, which allows England's Henry V to marry Catherine, daughter of France's Charles VI. The treaty also disinherits the French dauphin (son of King Charles VI and Queen Isabeau) and declares that the firstborn son of Henry V and Catherine will become king of France.

**1422**
Both Henry V and Charles VI die within two months of each other, and the successor to the French throne is uncertain. The English proclaim the infant Henry VI king, while the French declare the dauphin (Charles VII) to be king.

**1425**
Thirteen-year-old Joan starts hearing the voices of angels and saints giving her advice.

**May 1428**
Joan leaves Domrémy to ask Commander Robert de Beaudricourt in Vaucouleurs to give her an escort to see the dauphin, Charles VII. Beaudricourt refuses and she returns home.

**July 1428**
Domrémy is raided by Burgundian troops. Joan, her family, and other townspeople take refuge in Neufchâteau.

**January 1429**
Joan makes another trip to Vaucouleurs to ask Beaudricourt for his assistance. He turns her down again, but this time she does not return home. She waits.

**October 12, 1428**
In the absence of the Duke of Orléans, the English commence the siege of Orléans.

**February 12, 1429**
Beaudricourt finally agrees to provide her with an escort to accompany her to Chinon to see the dauphin.

**February 23, 1429**
The Maid meets the dauphin in Chinon, where Joan convinces Charles VII to give her a chance to help him.

**April 29, 1429**
Joan arrives at Orléans, where she is immediately loved by the populace for coming to their aid when all looked hopeless.

**May 8, 1429**
After a bitter battle over Les Tourelles, the English leave Orléans, and the siege is over. The first part of her mission has been completed, and Joan is triumphant.

**July 17, 1429**
The dauphin is crowned king in Reims and becomes Charles VII.

**September 8, 1429**
The Maid is hurt during an advance on Paris. The following day, King Charles VII forces her army to give up its quest, turning the setback into a failure.

**December 1429**
King Charles VII rewards Joan for her services to the country by granting her, her family, and their descendants nobility and the royal surname *du Lys* (Lily).

**May 23, 1430**
During a skirmish in Compiègne, the Maid is captured by Burgundians.

**November 21, 1430**
The Maid is sold by the Burgundians to the English for 10,000 francs. She is then taken to Rouen for trial.

**February 21, 1431**
Joan appears for the first time in front of her prosecutors for her condemnation trial. The trial is run by Burgundian supporters of England from the University of Paris.

**May 30, 1431**
Joan is executed by being burned at the stake. The condemnation trial verdict is overturned in 1456, declaring Joan innocent. She is canonized in 1920, officially becoming Saint Joan of Arc.

**1431**

# Defender of France

*I must go, and I must do this thing, because my Lord will have it so.*

Again, sixteen-year-old French peasant Jehanne (Joan) Romée heard the voice of Saint Michael the Archangel declare, "You must go to the aid of the king of France." She protested, "I am a poor girl who knows nothing of riding and warfare." How could *she* help the king, who was dangerously close to losing his country to the English army and its French supporters?

Like most medieval Europeans, Joan's religion—Catholicism—was an integral part of her life. People felt so close to their saints that hearing heavenly voices was not uncommon. Joan's voices were extraordinary, however, because they told her that she alone could save her country in its war with England

Once she became convinced of her mission, Joan left the safety of her home and journeyed across the embattled countryside to fight for the future of France. In doing so, she risked capture and even death.

Young Joan's courageous determination to be true to her saints, her God, her king, and her people is echoed by the loyalty she attracts even today from groups as varied as Catholics who hold her as their patron saint, artists for whom she is an inspiration, and French citizens who consider her their national hero.

# CHAPTER 1

# Childhood in a Land at War

*Although France would be lost by a woman,*
*a maiden should save it.*
—*Prophecy in France during the 1400s*

"Like heralds of a new joy," the roosters crowed long before dawn on the day Jehanne (Joan) Romée was born in the village of Domrémy on the border of the region of Lorraine, France. At least, so claimed a Domrémy resident named Lord Boulainvilliers. Witnesses to the actual day of her birth were hard to come by. The custom of the day was to have witnesses for a baby's christening, not the birth. No records were kept, but the only day that is mentioned for Joan's birth is the one Lord Boulainvilliers stated—January 6, 1412. Joan herself did not know her own birthday.

Joan was one of five children born to Jacques d'Arc and Isabelle Romée. She had three older brothers—Jacquemin, Jean, and Pierre—and a sister, Catherine. Joan's parents had a small farm, and her father Jacques was also a town official who collected taxes.

*Joan* is the English version of her French name—*Jehanne*. People of that era referred to her by many names. "In my country (Domrémy), people called me Jeanette (little Joan), but they called me Jeanne when I [left]," she explained later in life. She signed her letters *Jehanne*, and

A photograph of Jehanne (Joan) Romée's birthplace and childhood home in Domrémy, France. After Joan's death, the name of her hometown was changed to Domrémy-la-Pucelle in her honor.

when referring to herself, she often used the term *La Pucelle,* meaning "the Maid." The name *La Pucelle* caught on and was widely used to refer to Joan.

Surnames were not commonly used in the middle ages. Accordingly, Joan's father's surname is spelled differently in various medieval texts, including Darc, d'Arc, Dars, Darx, Dare, Tarc, Dart, and more. Joan's mother was awarded her surname (Romée) after making a pilgrimage, or holy journey, to a sacred shrine. Joan did not use a last name at all, although she said that if she were to do so, it would be Romée, because local custom was for girls to take their mothers' surname.

Although Joan called herself Jehanne la Pucelle, historians and record keepers would call her Jeanne d'Arc in France and Joan of Arc in English-speaking countries.

Isabelle taught Joan to sew and spin, which the young girl did very well. Joan would also help on the farm or tend cattle or sheep at times. Like most peasants of that time, Joan never learned to read or write as a child. She regularly wore a ring given to her by her parents, which was etched with three crosses and the names *Jhesus Maria* for Jesus Christ and his mother, Mary.

Here is an example of Joan's signature. The Maid dictated her letters, but she learned how to write her name so she could sign them herself.

Catholicism was the official religion of France during the 1400s, and Isabelle sought to raise Joan as a good Catholic. Isabelle would later describe her daughter as **pious** and good hearted: "Because the people suffered so much, she had a great compassion for them in her heart and despite her youth she would fast and pray for them with great devotion and fervor."

## The Armagnacs and the Burgundians

In the woods near Domrémy, there was a tree known as the Ladies' Tree or the Fairies' Tree, which was reputed to be a meeting place for a fairy and her love. The waters near the tree were said to have healing powers, and the towns' children liked to dance by the tree and leave flower garlands on its branches. When she was very young, Joan would sometimes sing, dance, or place garlands in the tree in honor of Mary. As she grew older, she became more serious and felt she had no time for such frivolities—certainly not while her country was at war with England—a war that came to be known as the Hundred Years' War.

In France, there were two warring factions: the Armagnacs, named after their French leader, Bernard d'Armagnac, and the

# The Hundred Years' War

Joan of Arc was born into a dangerous and ugly era of France. In addition to coping with devastating plagues and famine, the French people faced a grim war with England that had begun seventy-five years before her birth.

The conflict within the French royal family began when Charles IV, king of France, died in 1328 without leaving an heir to the crown. For hundreds of years, royal fathers had passed the crown to their sons, but the line of succession was broken. Now, more than one potential king was prepared to grab the crown.

The king of England, Edward III, believed he should rule France as well as England because he was the nephew of the dead king. But a native Frenchman and cousin to Charles IV was chosen instead. His name was Philip VI. England's Edward III then declared war on France and the Hundred Years' War began in 1337. By the time Joan of Arc was born, generations of French people had been suffering horribly from the war. More civilians had died than soldiers. Even in times of relative peace, farms and villages were plundered by their own country's out-of-work soldiers.

Foot soldiers and knights on horseback battle in this fifteenth-century French manuscript illumination of the Hundred Years' War.

This illustration from Andrew Lang's *The Story of Joan of Arc,* published in 1906, shows Joan hanging garlands on the Fairy Oak.

Burgundians. Domrémy was an Armagnac village. Being Armagnac meant that one sided with the kings of France against the English king and his French supporters, known as Burgundians. The Burgundians were named after the French region of Burgundy, which was home to their leader, Philip III, Duke of Burgundy. Domrémy was close enough to Burgundian territory that Joan's childhood was affected by the tension between the two groups.

Although she was not involved in conflicts herself, Joan saw her brothers come home with black eyes and bloody noses from

Philip III, Duke of Burguncy, the head of the Burgundians and the main French rival of the Armagnacs, is shown in this fifteenth-century manuscript illumination.

fighting with Burgundian children in a nearby town. She later said that her people were united in their hatred of Burgundy. Joan grew up in a divided France that had not known a strong ruler.

## A Woman Loses France

In 1420, when Joan was eight years old, France was ruled by the French king Charles VI and his wife Isabeau. Charles VI had the nickname Charles the Mad because he suffered from bouts of mental illness. Nevertheless, that year the king and queen signed an important document called the Treaty of Troyes, which promised that their daughter, Princess Catherine, would marry the English king Henry V and that Henry V and their future son would inherit the French throne.

This nineteenth-century engraving of Shakespeare's *Henry V* portrays the conclusion of the Treaty of Troyes, when the French princess Catherine is promised to England's king, Henry V.

It is believed that because of his mental illness Charles VI did not understand the consequences of this treaty—although his queen, who sided with the Burgundians, probably did. In signing the treaty, their son Charles was no longer heir to the French throne. An Englishman—Henry V or his son—would receive the honor instead.

A well-known French **prophecy** predicted that a woman would lose France and a maid would save it. It seemed the first part of the prophecy was coming true—Queen Isabeau had lost France through the Treaty of Troyes.

The English king Henry V hoped to inherit the kingdom of France once Charles VI died. However, events did not go entirely the way Henry V had hoped. He did marry the French princess, and they did have a son, *but* Henry V did not outlive Mad Charles VI—who died a few months after Henry's death in 1422.

*A well-known French prophecy predicted that a woman would lose France and a maid would save it.*

Now that Henry V of England and Charles VI were both dead, who would be king? Henry V's son, Henry VI, was only an infant. The young heirs—England's Henry VI and France's Charles, the dauphin (heir to the kingdom)—were both proclaimed to be the new king of France, but it was not clear who would actually sit on the throne in the end.

Henry VI was too young, and Charles could not be the authentic king until he had a coronation at Reims, where he could be **anointed** as king with the sacred oil. Legend stated that this sacred oil had been brought from heaven in a dove's beak to anoint Clovis, the first French king. However, there was one small problem—Reims was in the hands of the English army, and as such, no ceremony for the dauphin could be held there.

Would the second part of the prophecy come true? Would a maid be able to save France?

King Clovis, who lived c. 467–511, was the first king of France. This sixth-century engraving shows the influential king with the church in his hands and fleur-de-lys on his robe.

# Charles VII (1403–1461)

Charles VII, the dauphin, was born in 1403, the eleventh child of Charles VI and Isabeau of Bavaria. Charles VI had become mentally incompetent years before Charles VII's birth. With Isabeau siding with the Burgundians, who gave her a comfortable place to live, and Charles VII planning to marry into a family of Armagnac backers, mother and son found themselves on opposing sides of France's civil war.

Charles VII had four older brothers, so initially it did not seem as though he had much of a chance of becoming king, but all his brothers died young and left no children. The last of his brothers died in 1417 when Charles VII was fourteen. At that time, Charles VII was living at the court of his future mother-in-law, Yolande of Aragon. His mother, Isabeau, wanted him to return to her court, but Yolande reportedly answered, "We have not nurtured and cherished this one for you to make him die like his brothers or to go mad like his father, or to become English like you."

An image of Charles VII as a young man dressed in armor.

With the aid of Joan of Arc, Charles VII was officially crowned king in the city of Reims in 1429. In spite of his "do-nothing" policy, the Hundred Years' War came to a triumphant end, and he was called Charles the Victorious. Charles VII died of a painful illness and mistakenly believed that his oldest son, Louis XI, had poisoned him.

# CHAPTER 2

# Sacred Voices

*Since God had commanded it, had I had a hundred
fathers and a hundred mothers, and had I been a
king's daughter, I would have gone.*

In 1425, thirteen-year-old Joan was outside in the garden
the first time she heard the voice of a spirit speaking to
her. It was accompanied by a great light, and young Joan
was terrified. She did not know who was speaking to her
or why. Was it friend or foe?

The voice kept returning, and by the third visit, she
was sure it was the voice of an angel. Knowing that it was a
friendly visitor made Joan look forward to what she called
her *révélations*—messages revealing the will of God. As
much as she enjoyed hearing from and seeing her angels,
she kept the knowledge of their
visits private, not informing her
friends or family.

## Saintly Messages

Joan identified her first
visitor as the Archangel Michael,
an angel-warrior and the leader
of God's army—an appropriate

Artist Howard Pyle created this illustration
in 1904 of Joan of Arc sharing a private
moment of wonder with her saints.

# Good and Evil Spirits

During Joan of Arc's era, both the Catholic Church and the public believed that spirits visited people. "Who did not have visions in the Middle Ages?" wrote historian Jules Michelet. Joan said that even the dauphin "had had many apparitions and some beautiful revelations."

The important thing about seeing spirits, people believed, was whether they were from God or from Satan. If they were from Satan, they were not to be trusted, and their instructions were not to be followed.

The Church had developed questions that would help it decide whether the visions were of good or evil spirits. These questions were called the principles of *discretio spirituum*. These principles investigated both the spirits and the person they visited—asking questions such as whether the messages from the voices matched the Church's beliefs and whether following the voices' instructions would produce good results. Also, they inquired about whether the person receiving the vision was virtuous.

If the Church did not agree with the messages—and they thought the instructions of the voices would not produce positive results—they could say that the visions were from Satan rather than from God.

In medieval times, people imagined good and evil vying for human souls. This woodcut from 1486 presents God and Satan looking on as a man navigates an ocean of vices and sin.

Archangel Michael arrives with a message for Joan in this nineteenth-century engraving.

messenger to encourage Joan to take action in the war. He was also the chosen guardian angel of French kings, including the dauphin, who would later put the archangel on his war banner. At first, though, Archangel Michael did not speak of the war or of helping the young dauphin become king. The archangel told Joan to behave well, go to church often, and follow the advice of Saint Catherine of Alexandria and Saint Margaret of Antioch, whom he said would be coming to see Joan next.

These two saints were both popular **martyrs** who died rather than give up their beliefs. They were models of brave resistance, **piety**, and purity. "They spoke well and fairly, and their voices are beautiful—sweet and soft," Joan said of Saint Catherine and Saint Margaret.

Piety and purity went hand in hand when people dedicated themselves to God, such as by becoming a nun, monk, or other **devotee**, because they were expected not to divide their affections between God and a human by getting married. Seeing Saints Catherine's and Margaret's commitment inspired Joan to devote herself to being unmarried for as long as it pleased God. That was why she started calling herself the Maid—to emphasize her standing as a woman who was faithful to God.

After a year of advice about behaving well and attending church, the voices started telling Joan "about the pitiful state of the Kingdom of France" and that she needed to come to the aid of the man who should be king, Charles, the dauphin. Two and three times a week she was told to help the young prince. Joan told her saints that she was only a peasant girl who did not know anything about riding horses or fighting. She felt unequipped to lead, yet the voices insisted.

*She felt unequipped to lead, yet the voices insisted.*

Joan knew her parents would not want her to leave Domrémy and go among the soldiers on a dangerous fool's errand. Her father had dreams that his daughter would go off with soldiers, and he feared they would come true. Worried about his daughter, her father said he would rather drown her himself than have her go. Hearing this, she knew she definitely could not expect his help in undertaking her plans.

The messages from her voices were clear, however—she had a job to do. Joan believed, "since God had commanded me to go, I must do it. And since God had commanded it, had I had a hundred fathers and a hundred mothers, and had I been a king's daughter, I would have gone."

# Her First Step

With her voices constantly urging her to take action, Joan decided to meet Robert de Beaudricourt, Armagnac supporter and commander of the fortress of nearby Vaucouleurs. She needed his help to see the dauphin. The land between her home and Chinon, where the dauphin resided was too perilous for a young woman alone. She was not ready to make the journey to Chinon yet, however. She just wanted to send a message to the dauphin in order to tell him to stand fast—that help was coming.

Nothing was simple for Joan, though—not even seeing Beaudricourt. She had to have an escort to Vaucouleurs. So she arranged to visit her cousin's family with the goal of having her cousin's husband, Durand Laxart, take her to Beaudricourt.

This is a photograph of a portion of the remains of the Vaucouleurs castle. Joan traveled to Vaucouleurs to ask Robert de Beaudricourt to give her an escort her to see the dauphin.

Because her cousin was expecting a baby, it did not seem out of the ordinary that Joan would want to visit her.

She succeeded in convincing Laxart to take her to Beaudricourt by reminding him of the well-known prophecy that a maid would win back France after a woman had lost it. Queen Isabeau was the woman who many believed had lost France by making the English kings heir to the French throne with the Treaty of Troyes, and Joan proposed to be the maid who saved France. Laxart would be her faithful helper.

When Joan met Beaudricourt, she told him that the Lord intended for the dauphin to be king and "that she would make [Charles] King, in spite of his enemies, and would conduct him to his coronation." The maid with the wild claims did not win over Beaudricourt right away. He turned her down, telling Laxart to "take her back to her father and to box her ears." Joan did return home, but her voices still told her to see Robert de Beaudricourt, so she did not give up, although she could not try again right away.

During the summer of 1428, Domrémy was attacked by Burgundians, and Joan's family fled to the walled city of Neufchâteau, where they stayed with other refugees at an inn. Sixteen-year-old Joan, along with her good friend Hauviette, worked at the inn. When Joan and her family left Neufchâteau, a man accused Joan of reneging on a childhood agreement to marry him, and took her to court over it.

Perhaps Joan's parents had arranged for her betrothal, or perhaps Joan herself had made a promise as a young girl, but now she had no intentions of marrying—not after she had vowed to stay unmarried and carry out God's plans. So, she bravely went to the town of Toul to face an **ecclesiastical** court. No record of the trial exists, so history does not know what was said, but she was able to defend herself successfully and leave as a free woman.

## England's Strategy in France

Henry V's brother, John, Duke of Bedford, was the British military leader in France. On October 12, 1428, John made his move and laid **siege** to the walled city of Orléans. During this time, the city was surrounded by soldiers, who conducted periodic attacks and prevented the city from receiving food supplies from the outside. The duke hoped that eventually the citizens would be so hungry they would surrender.

According to military rules of conduct at that time, the city of Orléans should have been safe

This manuscript illumination from the fifteenth century shows the city of Orléans besieged by the English army.

from siege because the Duke of Orleans was absent, captured by the English during the Battle of Agincourt. In a leader's absence, enemy soldiers were supposed to leave his lands alone. However, John of Bedford knew that Orléans was vital to England's interests.

If it could capture the city, the English army would be in position to attack the dauphin's seat of government in Bourges, and the portions of France that were under French control would lose hope. Consequently, the English army surrounded Orléans and prepared to stay until its surrender. The dauphin Charles and France itself, needed help more than ever.

# CHAPTER 3

# A Peasant Girl Leads the Way

*Surrender to the Maid sent hither, by God the King of Heaven, the keys of all the good towns which you have taken and laid waste in France.*

In the winter of 1429, Joan returned to Vaucouleurs to again ask Robert de Beaudricourt for his help. "I must be with the king before mid-**Lent**, though I wear my legs to my knees on the road," she said. "For there is none in this world . . . who can restore the Kingdom of France. Nor is there any succor [aid] for it but from me. Far rather would I sit and sew beside my poor mother . . . [but] I must do this thing, because my Lord will have it so." Although Beaudricourt no longer suggested that Joan should have her ears boxed, he still refused to take her to see the dauphin.

Joan stayed on in Vaucouleurs, waiting for Beaudricourt to change his mind. While there, her presence in town did not go unnoticed. Her sincerity and determination made an impression on the townspeople, and they told others about the young woman who felt so strongly that she could help the king.

A young Armagnac knight known as Jean de Metz met Joan in the street one day and teasingly asked whether the king would be driven from France and they would all become English. She assured him that she could save the kingdom from such a fate, and he was won over by her sincerity. "Her words put me on fire, inspiring in me a love for her that was, I believe, divine."

The leader of Joan's native region, the Duke of Lorraine, heard reports about the Maid from people who thought she seemed exceptional. He was in poor health and hoped that Joan could ask her angels to heal him. Upon his request, Joan traveled to see the nobleman, who was the highest-ranking person she had met thus far. In

*". . . I must do this thing, because my Lord will have it so."*

typical fashion, Joan told him straightforwardly how she felt. She confessed that she could not improve his physical health but advised him to work on his spiritual health—including giving up his mistress. While the Duke of Lorraine was not ready to change his behavior, he was sufficiently impressed with Joan to provide her with money and a horse.

## Convincing Beaudricourt

The Maid returned to Vaucouleurs to ask Beaudricourt a third time for assistance. He finally gave in. Perhaps he was tired of having her wait around for him to agree. Perhaps he may have been influenced by the growing number of townspeople who believed that her mission really was from God. Perhaps what Joan revealed to him on February 12 may have changed his mind. She told him that the French army had suffered a defeat at Rouvray that day—even though word of the loss had not reached Vaucouleurs yet.

The Battle at Rouvray did indeed turn out to be a depressing defeat for France (and the Scottish troops who were helping them). This conflict, although at Rouvray, was actually intended to assist the besieged city of Orléans The French and Scottish armies

# Scottish Help for France

France and Scotland had an old alliance due to their shared hostilities with England. As many as 15,000 Scottish soldiers went to France between 1419 and 1424, and had a great victory against the English in 1421 at Baugé. However, the Scottish soldiers also plundered the French peasants and did not make themselves very popular among the people.

The Scottish troops suffered significant losses at the Battle of Verneuil (1424) and the Battle of the Herrings (1429). After the defeat of the Battle of the Herrings at Rouvray, there were not enough men to have an official "army of Scotland" fighting in the war anymore. However, there was a smaller group that kept going. Scottish bowmen guarded Joan and her soldiers as they traveled from Blois to the siege, and a number of Scottish officers were with the Maid when she was at Orléans. Norman Leslie, a Scottish monk who later wrote the *Book of Pluscarden*, a history of Scotland, stayed with Joan until her death.

The Scottish army fought on the side of the French during the Hundred Years' War. Here, Scottish knights (on the right) confront the English army at the Battle of Normandy, 1429.

attempted to seize a convoy of supplies heading south to the English army at Orléans. The fight, called the Battle of the Herrings because the supplies contained substantial amounts of fish, was a complete victory for the English and was the last time anyone tried to free Orléans before the Maid arrived. However, Joan's successful prediction of the defeat did make Beaudricourt wonder if she might be divinely inspired after all.

Beaudricourt decided to give Joan the escort she requested, but before she left, he had her **exorcised** by the parish priest as a precaution against her having been sent by the devil. The priest asked any evil spirits in Joan to leave and told her to step forward if she was good, which she did. The Maid was a bit offended by this as she had already visited the priest, and she believed he knew perfectly well she needed no exorcism. She went along with it anyway and received permission to go to the dauphin.

## On to Chinon

Before leaving, Joan cut her long hair and swapped her red peasant dress for male clothes, which were more appropriate for traveling and fighting.

As Joan and her companions, including her devotee Jean de Metz, left on February 12 for Chinon, Beaudricourt bid them, "Go, go, and let whatever good can, come of it." It took only eleven days for the group to cross 350 miles, including six rivers, and to reach Chinon castle, where the dauphin was residing.

During the journey, they traveled through enemy territory and were very careful not to get caught. They stopped to hear **Mass** in only two churches that they felt were safe to enter. At first, her escorts wondered if she was more arrogant than holy, and they thought about putting her to a test. Before they could devise one, they were touched by her sincerity and became "ready

In this painting by Jean-Jacques Scherrer (1855–1916), Joan is being given a sword and a message for the dauphin by Robert de Beaudricourt as she is about to set off for Chinon.

to do whatever Joan pleased and were as eager to present her to the King as [she was to see him.]"

As they neared Chinon castle, Joan crossed a drawbridge where a guard insulted her. The Maid remarked prophetically that someone who would be dying soon should not be behaving in ways that would upset God. The guard drowned later that day.

When Joan and her escorts arrived, the dauphin did not receive the Maid immediately. He knew she was coming as Beaudricourt had sent a letter telling him she was on her way.

Shown are the ruins of the castle at Chinon, where Joan traveled to see the dauphin.

The dauphin was not exactly sure what to do about her. She obviously wanted to help him, and she had favorably impressed his supporter Robert de Beaudricourt. However, her claims were outlandish, and he wondered if she could be an agent of the devil in disguise.

Some of his representatives came to question her and find out what she wanted. The Maid explained that her mission was to lift the siege of Orléans and to have the dauphin crowned king. Despite any misgivings the men continued to have, they did allow her to finally enter.

# What Did Joan Look Like?

Not much is known about Joan's appearance because there are no images of her from her lifetime other than a sketch drawn by a man who had never seen her. She is described as having dark hair. Her future **squire**, Jean d'Aulon, related that she was "beautiful and shapely." Later, nobleman Guy de Laval would write to his mother that seeing and hearing her was "entirely divine."

During her short military career, her image was said to have been painted and struck on medals commemorating her triumphs, but nothing remains. The descriptions of the armor she wore and the banner she carried have been the springboards for thousands of artists' depictions of her.

No one knows what the Maid really looked like, so artists imagine her many different ways. This profile portrait of Joan in her armor was painted in 1873.

# Tested and Tried

As Joan was led into Chinon castle to meet Charles, the dauphin, on the evening of February 23, 1429, she unknowingly underwent a test. The dauphin, instead of being in grand dress and sitting in the place of honor ready to greet her, was in ordinary clothes and standing in a crowd. Would she be fooled or would she prove to have inexplicable abilities?

The Maid had never met or seen Charles before, but she readily spotted him and approached, saying "Most noble dauphin, the King of Heaven announces to you by me, that you shall be anointed and crowned king in the city of Reims, and that you shall be his vice-regent in France." Her recognition was enough for the dauphin to be willing to grant her an audience (talk with Joan privately).

No one knows what was said between them, but Charles was willing to accept the Maid afterward. Some people thought she repeated to him the words of a private prayer he had made or gave him another sign that she was sent by God. Neither of them would ever tell.

The Maid passes the test of recognizing the real dauphin at the Chinon court in this nineteenth-century wood engraving.

Soon after her meeting with the dauphin, Joan encountered a nobleman who would become a good friend—John, Duke of Alençon, who was only twenty-three years old but had already spent five years as an English prisoner. He watched her practicing with a lance and was so impressed he gave her a horse. Alençon never doubted that the Maid was worth following.

A c. 1505 illustration depicts an armored Joan riding a white horse and carrying her banner.

In a surprising move, Joan reportedly asked Charles, the dauphin, for a gift—France itself. He is said to have reluctantly given it to her, and she had official paperwork drawn to that effect on the spot. She immediately offered the issue to God in prayer, and then upon finishing her prayers, returned the document to Charles. The meaning behind her actions was that the leader of France was really the king of heaven, and that Charles was acting on God's behalf.

Before the Maid could proceed with her mission, however, the dauphin still had to convince his counselors that she was not crazy or disreputable. He sent Joan to Poitiers, which was the religious, judicial, and intellectual capital for those loyal to the Armagnac cause, for what would become her second trial experience.

In Poitiers, Joan confidently withstood considerable questioning by prominent Armagnac clergy during the month of March. The clergy who interrogated Joan found her to be good and honest. After following the approved principles of *discretio spirituum*, the clergy concluded that the Maid's intentions were truly Christian.

## Preparing for War

Now that Joan had received a positive response in Poitiers, it was time to prepare for her advance on the besieged Orléans. On March 22, Joan dictated a letter, which would be sent to the Duke of Bedford, leader of the English forces in France, to ask for the siege of Orléans to end: "Render to the Maid here sent by God the King of Heaven, the keys of all the good towns which you have taken and violated in France. She is here come by God's will to reclaim the blood royal (rightful heir). . . . You, Duke of Bedford, the Maid prays and requires of you that you cause no more destruction to be done. . . . And make answer if you wish to make peace in the city of Orléans. And if you make it not, you shall shortly remember it, to your very great injury." An impressive warning, to be sure, but the English response was to hold the messengers captive.

*Joan went to the town of Tours to ready herself for the battle.*

Joan went to the town of Tours to ready herself for the battle. She sent a letter asking for a particular sword that was hidden near an altar at Saint Catherine's Chapel in Fierbois. It was not unusual for weapons to be left in churches because soldiers would

An undated illustration shows the Maid receiving the blessed sword of Saint Catherine.

offer them to Saint Catherine in thanks for her protection during combat. The Maid's voices had told her about a particular sword with five crosses upon it. It was, in fact, found and given to Joan. The churchmen said they rubbed it, and the rust came off immediately, revealing five crosses.

She was also outfitted in Italian-style white armor made especially to fit her small, female form. "White armor" indicates that it was plain, rather than highly decorated in the German style. Armor could only protect a fighter so much, though. While in Tours, the Maid predicted that she would be wounded at Orléans by an arrow above the breast, but not killed. Because she did not have any money of her own, Joan relied on donations from others for all her gear. Charles's mother-in-law, Yolande of Aragon, was an early supporter of Joan's and helped fund her campaign to save Orléans.

Banners held high were important in warfare: as focal points for rallying the troops, as morale boosters, and as ways to see that the fight continued. If the banner was down, the battle could be over. Accounts of Joan's banner vary. It is always described as a white banner with angels and fleur-de-lys (the royal symbol of lilies) on it, but the details change. Some say that the banner had angels holding fleur-de-lys; others say that the Lord was holding the world, flanked by angels on either side. The only words on it were *Jhesus Maria*. Joan would later say, "I loved [my] sword because it was found in the church of Saint Catherine, whom I loved. But I loved my banner forty times better than my sword. And when I went against the enemy, I carried my banner myself, lest I kill any."

Sword, armor, banner—now the Maid was ready for her first military move.

Shown is an artist's depiction of Joan's banner based on the Maid's descriptions.

# CHAPTER 4

# Lifting the Siege

*All is yours; enter!*

How dire was life under the siege? It was so grave that citizens of Orléans believed their only hope was a miracle. They remembered hearing about the English army's siege of Rouen, ten years earlier, when the desperate population had been driven to eat cats, rats, dogs, and horses before finally surrendering. The last attempt to help Orléans—the battle that Joan had predicted to Beaudricourt—had gone badly. Who would save them now?

The man in charge of defending Orléans in the absence of the Duke of Orléans (who was still a captive of the English army) was the duke's half-brother, John, who was known then as the Bastard of Orléans—a name that was not considered insulting. He had a faint glimmer of hope because he had heard a rumor in February about a maid who intended to lift the siege and lead the dauphin to Reims. Wanting to learn more about her, he sent messengers to

Joan's friend, John, Bastard of Orléans, Count of Dunois, is portrayed in this 1788 engraving.

Chinon to bring back information. They returned to say that, yes, there was such a young woman, and she had told the dauphin that she had come to achieve these miracles.

## Life as an Army Captain

The Maid had readied herself for battle and had written to the English again, asking them to leave Orléans. Her brothers Jean and Pierre had joined Joan, along with a priest that her mother had arranged to accompany her. Together with the entourage the dauphin had provided, she arrived at Blois on April 22 to join the rest of the army that was assembling there.

Joan immediately began shaping up the army. She insisted that the soldiers stop swearing and start going to church. She made sure that the troops did not bother the local civilians.

John, Duke of Alençon cursed frequently before joining the Maid, but, not wanting to quarrel with Joan, he said, "When I saw her, I refrained from my swearing." He commented, as did other soldiers, that the Maid was simple and uneducated in most ways, but "in the matter of war she was very expert, in the management of the lance and in the drawing up of the army in battle order and in preparing the artillery." Knight Thibault d'Armagnac said, "She behaved as if she had been the shrewdest captain in the world and had all her life been learning [the art of] war."

One of Joan's companions, Simon Beaucroix, described her as a leader who "never allowed any of her company to pillage because she never wanted food that she knew was stolen." These changes might have been unwelcome for some soldiers, but many appreciated having someone to believe in and responded positively to her efforts. The civilians whose farms were safer thanks to her were certainly grateful.

For the five-hundredth anniversary of the Maid's visit to Blois, the town erected a plaque that reads: "Joan of Arc arrived in Blois on April 25, 1429. She organized her army there and blessed her banner in the Church of Saint-Sauveur and left on the 27th of April to liberate Orléans."

Joan and the army left Blois on April 27 to travel to Orléans. She was met in Checy by John, the Bastard of Orléans, and other knights who were "right joyful at her coming." The Maid had planned how she wanted the army to approach Orléans, so she was not pleased two days later when the army arrived and she saw John had brought them to a different location. He had thought they would be safer there, but she said, "The counsel of the Lord your God is wiser and safer than yours. You thought to deceive me and it is yourself above all whom you deceive, for I bring you . . . [aid] from the King of Heaven."

Nearby, supply boats that the army had escorted to the city were sitting motionless, waiting for the wind to change. However, shortly after John's conversation with the Maid, the direction of the wind shifted. The supply boats could raise their sails and continue into Orléans. John felt this was a sign that Joan did have a touch of the divine about her, and he asked her to go into the walled city of Orléans "where she was greatly wished for."

After escorting her into the city, John went to Blois to bring reinforcements to the fight. From this point on, the two allies would get along very well.

## The Maid Enters Orléans

Although Orléans was mostly surrounded by English soldiers, there were unguarded spots where Joan could enter the walled city. Upon her entrance on April 29, 1429, the people of the city "felt already comforted, as though freed of the siege by the divine virtue that they were told resided in that simple Maid, whom they regarded with strong affection. . . . And there was a marvelous crowd pressing to touch her or the horse on which she rode."

Inside, Joan rode her horse around the city, encouraging the citizens. The streets were so full of people who had come to see her that she could hardly pass. When she was not cheering the populace, she viewed the opposition's layout and forces and spent time praying. She also called out to the enemy over the wall, exhorting them to leave or asking about her messengers who had not returned. The English answered back with insults, including one threat that they would burn her if she were ever caught.

On May 4, John of Orléans and the army arrived and began

In this painting, Jean-Jacques Scherrer captures the excitement of the people of Orléans upon the arrival of their beloved Joan of Arc.

Shown are the ruins at Saint-Loup, where Joan helped to bring victory over the English.

a skirmish, or a short-term fight, at the English-held Saint-Loup, about a mile away from Orléans. This tactic was a diversionary move that John hoped would allow supplies to enter the city, but the fighting became more serious than expected. Joan was resting in Orléans when she suddenly sensed that combat was taking place. She scolded her attendant for not telling her "the blood of France was spilling!" and she raced to Saint-Loup, bringing additional troops with her. When she arrived on the scene, the French soldiers cheered at the sight of her, and she urged them on to victory. Saint-Loup was in French hands again.

## Fighting the English

That same day, John told the Maid that he had heard additional enemy forces were coming to Orléans, headed by Sir John Fastolf, leader of the English during the Battle of the Herrings. Rather than being dismayed at the idea of reinforcements, Joan was delighted at the idea of confronting another enemy leader. She joked, "so soon as you know of the coming of the said Fastolf, you will let me know; for, if he pass without my knowing, I promise you I will have your head." Her friend replied that "of this he had no fear, for he would certainly let her know."

On May 5, the French troops waited because it was a religious holiday—**Feast of the Ascension Day** (the fortieth day after Easter). During the delay, Joan dispatched her final request to the English in an unconventional manner.

She tied a letter to the tip of an arrow and shot it into the enemy's camp. The Maid signed her letter "Jhesus Maria, Jehanne La Pucelle," and as something

*Inside, Joan rode her horse around the city, encouraging the citizens.*

of a "P.S." she included below her signature, "I would have sent you this letter in a more suitable manner, but . . . you have kept my herald Guyenne; I pray you to send him back, and I will send you some of your people who have been taken at the fort of Saint-Loup, for all were not killed there." The English responded by calling out a slur against her, and Joan, who preferred peace to violence despite her jokes about Sir Fastolf, wept that the siege could not be ended peacefully.

The next day, Joan insisted that they launch a sudden attack on the English forces. She met resistance from other war captains who wanted to wait, but she prevailed and headed to the fort of Saint-Jean-le-Blanc with troops. They found Saint-Le-Blanc abandoned by the English army, which had gathered at Les Augustins. A subsequent attack on Les Augustins was ultimately successful, and the day ended with two forts once again in French hands. During the fighting, Joan stepped on a caltrop, a type of spiked iron weapon. Although she was seen limping, the wound was not serious. However, she told her priest, Jean Pasquerel, that the next day, "blood will flow from my body, above my breast."

## The Heart of the English Strongholds

On May 7, the French captains once again wanted to be cautious and wait, but Joan, backed by popular sentiment in

An undated image portrays the injured Maid at the battle for Orléans. The artist evokes the chaos of the fighting and the deep concern of Joan's fellow soldiers.

Orléans, sought immediate action. Her goal: Les Tourelles—two towers that were the heart of the English strongholds that encircled the city. The fighting at Les Tourelles commenced early in the morning. At about noon, when Joan was climbing a ladder against a wall, she was pierced by an arrow between her neck and shoulder. The wound was deep—perhaps six inches. The tip might have even stuck out of her back.

The Maid had to be carried out of the fighting. Sir Gamaches, a knight who had previously argued about taking orders from a peasant girl and called Joan a "little saucebox," brought her to safety. She pulled out the arrow on her own, and the wound was dressed with the usual treatment—olive oil and bacon fat. The Maid rejected soldiers' offers to say charms (magical verses) over her injury as she considered them ungodly.

The English soldiers thought she might be dead, and the French troops were worried. The French continued to fight, but were not making progress. John of Orléans considered calling a halt to the offensive, but Joan asked him to wait before ordering a retreat. She told the soldiers to rest and eat while she went to pray.

A section of a mural at the Panthéon in Paris depicts Joan waving her banner and encouraging her weary soldiers to advance and win Orléans.

A short while later, the Maid returned. Despite her wound, she led a fresh assault on Les Tourelles. The sight of Joan's banner waving vigorously and leading the way heartened the troops, and they were able to achieve total victory. "All is yours; enter!" called Joan once her banner touched the fortress. Inside the city, bells rang and people sang "Te Deum laudamus" ("We praise thee, O God") to celebrate the triumph. The Maid and others spent the night in the fields to protect the city from any possible counterattack from English troops.

The night was quiet, but the next day, the English forces arranged themselves in battle formation. The French troops came out to meet them but did not fight. Joan had forbidden that they start any combat that day because it was Sunday but told them that they could defend themselves to the best of their abilities. The French soldiers would have preferred to war with the English army, but they restlessly held back. After about an hour of being in close proximity with each other, the English forces turned and left. The liberation of Orléans was complete!

# English Leaders at the Siege

The head of the English army at Orléans was John Talbot, First Earl of Shrewsbury, who fought in Wales and Ireland before coming to France. After being captured in Rouen in 1449, he agreed to never take up arms against Charles VII again. William Glasdale was the captain of the fort at Les Tourelles. As the French were making their final advance on Les Tourelles, Joan yelled to Glasdale to surrender to the King of Heaven, but he rejected her call with insults. Shortly thereafter, the captain fell into the Loire River in his armor and drowned. Joan lamented his and the other English deaths.

British leader John Talbot led the English army at Orléans.

# CHAPTER 5

# More Battles for the Maid

*Fille-Dé [child of God], go, go, go; I will be at your aid, go.*

—One of Joan's voices

On the day the English left Orléans, the townspeople had a procession to celebrate their deliverance and to honor the Maid. The city would continue to have such celebrations every May 8 thereafter—except for the years they were forced to halt them during the French Revolution. Joan's ideals of **chivalry** and good behavior by the army were a refreshing change for the citizens of Orléans. Unlike before, they did not have to fear the Maid's army.

Always eager to press on, Joan did not stay long to enjoy the victory. She and John of Orléans rode toward Tours to join the dauphin and to discuss their next steps. Accounts of the lifting of the siege spread like wildfire. Before Joan's arrival, Charles received so many messengers with updates that he had to keep adding on to the letter he was writing to let his loyal subjects know the good news.

The news also spread through the English and Burgundian side as well. On May 10, Clément de Fauquembergue, a clerk of the Burgundian-ruled Parliament in Paris, made note of the Orléans events and drew a little sketch of Joan. That drawing, although done without his ever actually having seen the Maid, is the only picture of her produced during her lifetime that still exists.

Although artist Clément de Fauquembergue never saw the Maid, this sketch detail by him is the only surviving drawing of Joan made during her lifetime.

Joan's deeds captured the imagination of all who heard of her; even people in other countries, such as Italy, thought a miracle had occurred. Supporters of the Armagnacs expected great things from the Maid. Conversely, a strong desire to be rid of her filled the **Anglo-Burgundians**. Many considered her a witch, while others looked at her with awe. Rumors grew that soldiers saw white butterflies fluttering around her banner wherever she carried it. Because butterflies were a Christian symbol of rebirth—the caterpillar reborn as a butterfly—the rumors meant that Joan really might have special heavenly powers.

## Clearing the Way for the Dauphin

Now that the tide had finally turned, the question was, what to do next? The English expected that the French militia, or army, would almost immediately advance on them in either Normandy or Paris. Joan, however, was determined to keep to her original plans—first free Orléans, which she had accomplished, then crown the king. It was an audacious strategy because Reims, where the coronation had to take place, was much farther away than Paris, and they would need to regain many towns from the enemy along the way. When Joan became frustrated that the dauphin's counselors did not seem to believe her approach was what God intended, she prayed about it, and was happy to hear a voice say, "Fille-Dé [child of God], go, go, go; I will be at your aid, go." The Maid convinced her dauphin to follow her lead, and an army of about seven thousand men was gathered for the campaign.

Among the nobles who joined the Maid's army were Guy and André de Laval. The young men were the grandsons of Anne de Laval, the widow of Bertrand du Guesclin—a hero of Joan's. He had been the military commander and **constable** of France and had successfully won back portions of France in the second phase of the Hundred Years' War that had been lost to England in the early years of the war.

Joan sent Anne a small gold ring out of respect and as a "pledge that she was carrying on the great and holy cause of France's peace and freedom." In a letter, Guy described the soldiers' enthusiasm to his mother and grandmother:

> *The Maid convinced her dauphin to follow her lead, and an army of about seven thousand men was gathered for the campaign.*

"They say that the king has never had such a great army as the one expected here; and never has there been stronger will for the task that they undertake here."

## The Battle of Jargeau

On June 10, Joan and the army, which included John, Duke of Alençon (the head of the army and highest ranking noble present), John of Orléans, and La Hire, a military commander who had fought at Orléans, headed for the town of Jargeau. John of Orléans had already attempted to take Jargeau in May but

This illustration from *The Chronicles of Jean Froissart,* a French history completed in 1400, depicts the siege of a castle using crossbows and cannons—not unlike the weapons used at the Battle of Jargeau.

failed. When they arrived on June 11, the French leaders were uncertain about another military attempt, but the Maid rallied them with the assurance that "if she were not secure in the knowledge that God was overseeing this work, she would have preferred to watch over the sheep rather than expose herself to such perils." On the second day of the fighting, Joan, who had promised the Duke of Alençon's wife to let no harm come to him, saved the duke's life. The Maid pointed at a cannon on the rampart and told Alençon to move from where he was standing in order to avoid being hit. Immediately after he left the spot, he witnessed the weapon kill an unlucky soldier who had just come to the same location.

Later that day, Joan faced injury herself but surged ahead. As she started climbing a ladder against the town walls, an English soldier threw a large stone or cannonball, which ripped through her banner and hit her head, knocking her to the ground. She rose unharmed and encouraged the Frenchmen to seize the moment. They took Jargeau completely after that. The English leader at Jargeau—William de la Pole, the fourth earl and first duke of Suffolk—is said to have asked for Joan to be the one to capture him, but when that did not happen, he knighted the French soldier who apprehended him, as he was too ashamed to be taken by a commoner.

On June 13. the Maid was back in Orléans, where she was presented with a gift on behalf of the city's still-imprisoned leader, the Duke of Orléans. It was a luxurious robe and coat tailored from his family's colors with the d'Orléans symbol (nettle leaves) woven into them. Although appreciative, Joan was not one to stay long when there was work to be done, and this time was no exception.

She and the army left two days later to take the bridge of Meung-sur-Loire. Shortly thereafter, Joan's army attacked the English troops at the city of Beaugency, and on June 17, Beaugency was won.

A statue of Joan holding her banner commemorates the liberation of Beaugency in 1429.

## The Battle of Patay

The next battle to be fought would take place at Patay, a town in north-central France. John Talbot, the English leader at the siege of Orléans, was in command of the English army for this battle. Also present was Sir John Fastolf, who had fought in Henry V's campaigns.

The French army under Joan of Arc was joined by Arthur de Richemont, the current constable of France, and his forces. Richemont's arrival was controversial because he had fallen out of the dauphin's good graces due to his brother's alliance with the English. Nevertheless, Richemont greeted the Maid in a straightforward manner and said, "I do not know if you are from God or not. If you are from God I fear nothing from you, for God knows my good-will. If you are from the Devil, I fear you even less." Joan welcomed him courteously, and they made ready for battle.

Constable of France Arthur de Richemont joined Joan's army at the Battle of Patay.

On the night of June 17, the two opposing armies were encamped close enough that they could actually see each other. English messengers approached the French and were told by Joan, "Go to your quarters for today, for it is rather late. But tomorrow, if it please God and Our Lady, we shall take a closer look at you." Although the English troops were outnumbered, they were still confident because they had been outnumbered at some of their most successful battles. This time, however, events would go differently.

It was a tense night, and the Duke of Alençon asked Joan her advice about how to handle the fighting in the morning. "Have all good spurs," she recommended. Spurs were used to encourage a horse to run faster, so the men present asked if she was suggesting that they were going to have to run away. She answered that it was not they who would be running away but the English, and "you will have need of good spurs as you chase after them." The Maid told the French troops that victory was assured: "Go at [the English] boldly. [Even] if they were in the clouds, we should have them."

*. . . the two . . . armies were encamped close enough that they could actually see each other.*

As it turned out, the French did chase after the English, who had broken camp early in the morning. The French army went searching for their foes, who were hiding in the forest. Suddenly, a stag jumped into the midst of the English troops. Surprised, the soldiers called out a hunting cry. Not realizing the French army was nearby, the English troops had inadvertently given away their location.

When the battle started, the English soldiers were disorganized and unable to use the techniques that worked for them in the past. The French armored knights slaughtered the

An artist's rendering of the Battle of Patay shows the banners of the French army decorated with the royal symbol of the fleur-de-lys.

**longbow** men. Although the Maid always preferred to be at the head of their offensives, she was in the rearguard on this occasion, and much of the fighting was done by the time her forces arrived.

The French were able to defeat the English decisively. The English army lost more than half of its soldiers; the English commander John Talbot was captured; and Sir John Fastolf ran away. The Duke of Alençon, perhaps thinking of his days as a captive of the English, asked his new prisoner John Talbot if he had realized this morning what would happen to him before sunset. Talbot replied, "It is the fortune of war." The fortune of war had smiled on Joan of Arc, but how much longer would it last?

# Sir John Fastolf (birth unknown–1459)

Thinking the battle was hopeless, Sir John Fastolf left the fighting at Patay and, with a small band of men, headed to Paris. The Duke of Bedford, leader of the English army in France, was so angry with Fastolf for abandoning the battle that he took Fastolf's title away. After an investigation into the incident, however, Fastolf was reinstated into the Order of the Garter (knighthood) and Talbot was actually blamed for the loss at Patay. Fastolf returned to his leaders' good graces and continued serving in France, although the taint of cowardice would follow him.

In William Shakespeare's play *Henry VI, Part 1* (circa 1589), Shakespeare includes Joan of Arc's campaigns, presenting Sir John as a coward and the Maid as a promiscuous witch. Later when Shakespeare wrote *Henry IV, Parts 1* and *2* (he did not write his historical plays in chronological order), he named one of his characters "Sir John Falstaff." This Falstaff character, a fainthearted, comedic glutton, was actually based on John Oldcastle, a fifteenth-century Englishman; the character was initially named Oldcastle. However, when Oldcastle's relatives complained, Shakespeare changed the name to Falstaff, thereby creating an association with the unfortunate Fastolf.

Many people mistakenly associated Shakespeare's Falstaff from *Henry IV* with John Fastolf, the Englishman who fled from the Battle of Patay.

# CHAPTER 6

# Crowning the King

*The rightful King of France, who has long suffered many a great misfortune . . . now approaches . . . coming as a crowned King in might and majesty, wearing spurs of gold . . .*

—Christine de Pisan, poet

The Battle of Patay marked the end of the fighting along the Loire River (known as the Loire Campaign): the region around the river had been freed from English control. The English leaders anticipated that the French army would go to Paris next—but that would not be the case. Joan was eager to get to Reims for the dauphin's coronation, but again, things moved slower than she had hoped.

There would be more encounters before they reached Reims, but the dauphin dragged his heels every time Joan wanted to take action. Now as the army gathered at Gien, Charles and his counselors hesitated to continue their journey. Enguerrand de Monstrelet, a Burgundian historian, described the dauphin as a man who "had no heart for war if he could do without it." Granted, a Burgundian supporter might be expected to think ill of the dauphin, but he seems to have accurately summed up Charles.

The French army, which had been paid poorly, was still willing to go wherever Joan led them. While the Maid was impatiently waiting for Charles to permit them to leave, she took this time to dictate a letter to Philip III, Duke of Burgundy, asking him to unite with Armagnacs and disavow his allegiance to England. However, Phillip's ties to England were made strong by his sister Anne's marriage to John, Duke of Bedford.

The dauphin also sent letters to nobles, asking them to attend the coronation. Even though he was slow to move, he was hopeful that he could successfully journey to Reims and officially be crowned king. Anxious to get going, Joan and others started for Reims and traveled for two days before the dauphin finally decided to follow her.

*Joan was eager to get to Reims for the dauphin's coronation . . .*

Their first stop along the way was Auxerre, a town which had a Burgundian garrison (body of troops) stationed there. The townspeople did not offer their allegiance to the dauphin, but they said they would give him the same level of obedience he received from certain other cities—namely Troyes, Châlons-sur-Marne, and Reims.

## The Challenge of Troyes

The next two towns that the group passed—Saint-Florentin and Saint-Phal—accepted Charles willingly, but no one was sure what would happen at Troyes—the town where the infamous Treaty of Troyes (which had made Henry V the heir to the French throne) had been signed. The townspeople were concerned that Charles would want to wreak vengeance upon them for being the source of his misfortunes. Charles and Joan had both sent letters to the town, promising them safety, but when the Armagnacs arrived, the gates to Troyes were shut against them.

The French army spent days waiting outside the city. Its supplies had dwindled, and it did not have much food left. Fortunately, the previous year a Franciscan **friar** named Brother Richard had urged the farmers of Troyes to plant more beans than usual, telling them "the one who must come will come soon." Consequently, there were lots of beans for the soldiers to eat but, unhappily, no pots for cooking them.

As the dauphin and his counselors fretted (again) about their ability to prevail, Joan organized an attack. She instructed the soldiers where to go, arranged for them to collect wood to fill the moat, and determined where to put the cannons and ladders. Her skill and ease with military planning impressed the other army captains.

Once Joan's army was ready for an attack, the frightened people of Troyes sent messengers to negotiate a peaceful solution.

The present-day town of Troyes is shown in this photograph.

An agreement was reached. The English and Burgundian soldiers would leave the city unharmed, which they did on July 10. However, when the enemy soldiers tried to take their Armagnac prisoners with them—having viewed the captives as their possessions—Joan refused to let them go and convinced the dauphin to pay for the release of the prisoners. Now, Charles entered the city victoriously.

Two days later, the dauphin and his army proceeded to Châlons-sur-Marne, where they were greeted warmly. In Châlons, Joan saw her godfather and other old friends from Domrémy, who were making their way to Reims for the coronation.

The army's next stop was Sept-Saulx, a town about halfway in between Châlons and Reims, leaving them with eight miles to go before the dauphin could become the king. Charles was uncertain what his reception at Reims would be. If the town chose to fight—which England's Duke of Bedford had been expecting it would—Charles doubted that his forces had the strength to win. However, Joan reassured him that Reims would open its doors to him and said that if "he would advance courageously he would recover all his kingdom."

## Coronation in Reims

As it turned out, a delegation from Reims came to Sept-Saulx to offer their allegiance, and the dauphin did not meet with any resistance at all. Burgundian-supporters hurried out of the area before the French army entered on July 16. Charles, the dauphin, was greeted with cries of "Noel! Noel!" a traditional greeting for new kings that might have dated from the Christmas coronation of King Charles I (also known as Charlemagne).

To Joan's joy, her father and possibly her mother went to Reims to see the dauphin be anointed. In honor of the Maid, the

In this undated drawing, Joan of Arc escorts the dauphin into Reims for his coronation.

town paid for their lodging while they were there. Certainly, this was a special occasion for the father who had worried so about his daughter leaving home. Durand Laxart, the cousin's husband who had helped Joan with the first stage of her journey, also went to Reims for the event. Townspeople held Joan in such esteem that they wanted to touch her ring or have her hold their religious objects. She did not believe that her touch actually conferred anything holy onto the objects, but she was kind and generous and accommodated those she met.

After rapid preparations, the dauphin was crowned on July 17 in a ceremony befitting a French king. Every aspect of the ceremony was handled in the ancient way so that there could be no doubt that the new king—now called Charles VII—and no other, was the legitimate ruler. Four chief nobles were charged with bringing the sacred anointing oil to the Cathedral of Notre

A panel from Jules Eugène Lenepveu's *Legende de Jeanne d'Arc* (Legend of Joan of Arc) depicts Joan standing by Charles VII during his coronation.

Dame in Reims from the abbey in Saint Rémy. The four lords carried their banners as they rode on horseback, escorting an abbot who walked between them as he carried the dove-shaped vial created especially to hold the holy oil.

The politics of war forced the dauphin to have participants in the ceremony that would not have joined him otherwise. Because his enemy lords and bishops would not pledge their allegiance to him, substitutes were found. The Duke of Alençon took the place of Philip III, Duke of Burgundy, and knighted Charles VII. Being knighted was important because knights were the protectors of the country, and the king was the symbolic leader of the knights. The new knight took an oath to defend and protect his people,

# Christine de Pisan (1364–c. 1430)

Armagnac poet Christine de Pisan (also known as de Pizan) escaped from Paris when the Burgundians captured the city in 1418. She came out of retirement during 1429 to compose the only major poem about Joan of Arc that was written during the Maid's lifetime. She completed *Le Ditie de Jehanne d'Arc (The Song of Joan of Arc)*, on July 31, 1429, only two weeks after Charles VII's coronation. Her poem gives readers a sense of the feelings of Armagnacs during that time. She wrote,

> "In 1429 the sun began to shine again. It brings back the good, new season which had not really been seen for a long time—and because of that many people had lived out their lives in sorrow; I myself am one of them. But I no longer grieve over anything, now that I can see what I desire . . .

> "The reason is that the rejected child of the rightful King of France, who has long suffered many a great misfortune . . . now approaches . . . coming as a crowned King in might and majesty, wearing spurs of gold . . .

> "And you, blessed Maid, are you to be forgotten, given that God [honored] you so much that you untied the rope which held France so tightly bound? Could one ever praise you enough for having bestowed peace on this land humiliated by war?"

The poet Christine de Pisan captured the spirit of the Maid in her verses.

and was dressed in the royal shoes adorned with the golden spurs of knighthood. After Charles VII's anointing, the bishops placed the crown upon his head and the deed was done. Charles VII was now the king of France.

The whole ceremony took about five hours, during which time Joan stood by the king holding her banner. When it was over, the Maid cried happy tears, as did many people in the cathedral. Joan had accomplished her mission: her country had a genuine French king.

Armagnacs across the country rejoiced. Poet Christine Pisan wrote *The Song of Joan of Arc* to celebrate the occasion. In her poem, she even mentioned the spurs of knighthood that symbolized Charles VII's status as the official king. However, the English government would not recognize Charles VII as the leader of France—they still wanted the English boy-king Henry VI to be king of France, and the Burgundians continued to side with the English. The war was not over yet.

> *After Charles VII's anointing, the bishops placed the crown upon his head and the deed was done.*

# CHAPTER 7

# On to Paris

*The place could have been taken!*

After the coronation ceremony, King Charles VII bestowed gifts on those who had helped him, including the Maid. Her request to the king was actually a favor for her home parish (church community). She asked Charles VII to free Domrémy and its neighboring village, Greux, from having to pay taxes. He agreed to her wish, and for hundreds of years—until the French Revolution—the official tax entries for Greux and Domrémy noted that their taxes were zero due to the Maid.

On the day of the coronation, Joan's thoughts turned again to peace. The Maid always sought peaceful solutions first, which is why she sent letters to the English officers before battling them in Orléans and why she wrote again now to Philip III, the Duke of Burgundy. She wrote, "Prince of Burgundy, I pray you, I entreat you, I beseech you as humbly as lieth [lie] in my power, that ye make war no more against the holy realm of France, and that forthwith and speedily ye withdraw those your men who are in any strongholds and fortresses of the said holy kingdom."

## A Temporary Truce

Joan did not personally receive a reply from the Duke of Burgundy, but the duke and the king did discuss a temporary truce. Unfortunately, Charles VII had trouble advancing his cause, even when things were going his way.

He feared action, preferring to take the easiest path possible, which was often doing nothing. To make matters worse, he listened to his counselor Georges de La Trémoïlle, who did not have the best interest of Armagnac at heart

The king and the duke arranged for a fifteen-day truce, after which the Burgundian leader claimed he would turn Paris over to Charles VII. Instead of making plans to leave Paris, however, the Anglo-Burgundian forces spent their time fortifying their defenses of it. Joan was not very happy about the agreement because she instinctively believed the Duke of Burgundy would not free Paris and that precious time was being wasted. She agreed to keep the truce at this time in order to preserve the king's word and honor.

In August of 1429, the Maid spoke with the Archbishop of Reims about her future plans. She told him how much she liked Reims, saying how happy she would be "when I shall end my days, as to be buried in the earth of this place!" The

*She agreed to keep the truce . . . in order to preserve the king's word and honor.*

archbishop asked Joan if she knew where she would die. She answered, "Wherever it may please God, for I am no more sure of the hour or the season or the place than you. And would that it were pleasing to God my maker that I might now turn back, laying off my arms, and go to serve my father and my mother, keeping their sheep with my sister and my brothers; they would be very glad to see me!"

At this point, Joan's heavenly mission—freeing Orléans and anointing Charles VII as king—had been completed. It was an opportune time for the Maid to return home, especially because the king could not be counted on to make good choices. However, Joan believed that the duke had lied to her king and

# The Maid's Sword

Many people had heard the story of Joan's Saint Catherine de Fierbois sword and how she had called for the weapon to be brought out of its hiding place. It was considered to be a holy sword. In the summer of 1429, though, rumors spread that the Maid had broken the Saint Catherine sword when she hit a prostitute on the back, trying to chase her away from the encampments.

Witnesses gave conflicting accounts about whether Joan actually did hit a prostitute across the back with a sword or if she just gave her a stern talking-to, but either way, the Maid said her Saint Catherine sword was never broken. She maintained that she gave the weapon to her brothers when she passed along her most precious belongings in spring 1430. Even though the Maid contradicted the rumor, there was still a tinge of fear among some soldiers and civilians that Joan's luck had run out with the breaking of the sword.

An engraving of the Maid shows Joan with her precious sword.

this so-called temporary truce was a false truce. Knowing that peace had not been restored in Paris, and that her good knights were eager to continue, Joan decided to make her way to Paris with her army.

## Making Their Way to Paris

As they traveled a meandering route to Paris, Burgundian-held towns, such as Soissons, Laon, Château-Thierry, and Provins, surrendered to the Armagnacs. Times were hard, though, for the underfed army and for the common people, who feared that the English army would punish them for allying with the king. The historian Monstrelet wrote that many more towns and castles farther into Burgundian territory would have willingly accepted the king had he brought his full forces to them, but Charles VII and his advisers were hoping a peace treaty with Philip III would make that unnecessary.

Charles VII foolishly continued to believe that peace might come about—even after he received word from England's Duke of Bedford that he considered Charles to be a false king. On August 7, the duke wrote a scathing letter to Charles VII asking him and Joan to come to them: "You Charles of Valois who . . . without cause call yourself King, that because you have wrongfully made new attempts against the Crown and lordship of the most high and excellent prince, my sovereign lord, Henry by the grace of God natural and rightful King of the kingdoms of France and England . . . and you are aided by superstitious and damnable persons, such as a woman of disorderly and infamous life, dressed in man's clothes and of

*Knowing that peace had not been restored in Paris, . . . Joan decided to make her way to Paris with her army.*

immoral conduct . . . Appear on this day and in this place, in person, bringing the deformed woman . . . and all the perjurers and other force that you wish and can muster." The duke asserted that God would support the English people because they were the only ones who really wanted peace for France.

On August 14, the duke and the Maid, along with their respective armies, approached each other near the town of Senlis, but no real fighting took place—only some skirmishes. Joan rode forward with the Duke of Alençon and called for the English soldiers to come out, but they refused, and eventually both sides separated without a battle. The English army headed for Paris, and the town of Senlis switched allegiances from the Burgundian to the Armagnac side.

Although there was not a big battle at Senlis, the town memorialized Joan with this statue and plaque.

# The King's Negotiations

Other shifts in allegiances that took place included Saint-Denis, which the Armagnac army took, and Beauvais, which willingly opened its gates to the French king. However, the Bishop of Beauvais, Pierre Cauchon, was not pleased because he was Burgundian, and had recently fled Reims rather than participate in the king's coronation.

The town of Compiègne also offered its loyalty to the king, but during the August peace talks, the Duke of Burgundy asked that it remain in Burgundian hands. Surprisingly, Charles VII consented to the duke's wishes—against the wishes of his own loyal people. The king seemed inclined to offer the duke anything in exchange for peace. He did not have the heart for war, and his funds were in short supply as well. Perceval de Cagny, who kept a record of events for the Alençon family, described the king's attitude: "it seemed from his manner that he was satisfied at that time with the mercies which God had granted him, without undertaking anything else."

As the French army pressed on to Paris, Charles VII and

A pen-and-ink drawing of Bishop Pierre Cauchon's tomb. Known also as the Bishop of Beauvais, Cauchon worked against Joan until the very end.

*Tombeau de marbre noire dans la Chapelle de Nôtre Dame de l'Église Cathédrale de Lisieux, de Pierre Cauchon Éveq.t de Beauvais en 1420. Et de Lisieux en 1432 mourut en 1442. Il portoit D'azur à une Croce D'arg.t &c. Cueilles Hor. 2. 81. Gallia Christiana. t. 2. s. 402. et 654. Il faut les prenere pour les mains*

his advisers, including Trémoïlle, lagged behind and met in Arras with representatives of the Duke of Burgundy. The fifteen-day truce period had expired and Paris was not handed over to the king. The failure of the Anglo-Burgundians to live up to their pledge to release Paris should have made the king mistrust future promises, but instead, the Armagnacs—without actually gaining anything or obtaining any promises from the Burgundian side—agreed to another truce from September 28 to Christmas.

## The Assault on Paris

Meanwhile, Joan carefully surveyed the territory around Paris. She determined that the Parisians were not about to open the city's gates for the king. Anglo-Burgundians had driven out or killed many of the Armagnac supporters in 1418, and those that were still loyal to the king inside the city dared not speak out.

Although Joan's saints had not told her whether the timing was right for a battle in Paris, French noblemen were encouraging her to make a move. The Maid decided she would enter the city once the king had arrived. She was eager to begin the attack, but Charles VII did not reach the city until September 7. Unfortunately, September 8 was a holy day, the Feast of the Birth of the Virgin Mary—certainly not a promising day for God-fearing Catholics to begin a battle—but begin they did. The combat started at midday. Paris was well fortified with walls as high as twenty-five feet. During the afternoon, in an attempt to cause confusion and panic, agents of the king yelled inside the city's

*The Maid decided she would enter the city once the king had arrived. She was eager to begin the attack, but Charles VII did not reach the city until September 7.*

An undated drawing shows Joan leading the battle for Paris.

walls that Paris had been taken and all was lost. This ploy was fairly successful, but trouble arose in the evening, as Joan led the way near Paris's Saint-Honore Gate.

Trying to determine the best way to cross the water moat, the Maid thrust her lance into the water to gauge its depth. She immediately became a clear target for the arrows that were pouring down around her. Suddenly one found its way into her leg, piercing straight through her thigh. Having lost a great deal of blood, she was carried away, all the while protesting that, "The place could have been taken!"

The next day, the Maid was eager and ready to continue their push on the city. She was cheered when she heard that a nobleman from Montmorency who had been against the king had left Paris that morning, along with fifty or sixty other gentlemen, to join the Armagnacs. Then she and her captains received word

Joan offered up her armor at a chapel in Saint-Denis. Shown is the Saint-Denis basilica, a historically important church, which is the burial site for 43 kings and 32 queens.

that Charles VII had decided to end the attack after just one day. The English had been willing to spend months to conquer a strategic city, such as Orléans, but Charles VII only gave the assault on Paris a day to succeed.

As unfair as it might seem, the failed charge on Paris was perceived as a sign of weakness on Joan's part. Previously, she had always succeeded at whatever she had set out to accomplish, but not this time. As was the custom of soldiers when they were wounded, the Maid made an offering in the chapel of Saint-Denis of a set of armor she had won in battle. In a way, it seemed as though she was hanging up her armor forever.

On September 21 at Gien, Charles VII commanded that the army, which he had been struggling to pay, be sent home. In his record of the events of the day, the Duke of Alençon's chronicler, Perceval de Cagny, wrote, "And thus were the will of the Maid and King's army broken."

# CHAPTER 8

# Changing Times

*He [the Duke of Burgundy] has, for some time, amused and deceived us by truces and otherwise, under the shadow of good faith.*
   —*Charles VII*

That same fall in 1429, some of the Armagnac war captains began to plan for battle again. When John of Alençon requested that the king send Joan with him, the less-than-loyal Trémoïlle tried to keep Alençon and the Maid apart by putting Joan in the care of his half-brother, Charles d'Albret. While waiting to be given an assignment, the Maid stayed in various homes, biding her time.

During that time, Joan met a woman named Catherine de la Rochelle who claimed she saw visions and had revelations like the Maid, but Joan believed the woman was full of "folly." The Maid met another visionary named La Pierrone as well; however, Joan seemed to accept this woman's experiences as genuine.

At about the time young Henry VI was being crowned king of England (November 1429), the Maid was finally given the opportunity to return to military action, although she was not allowed to go wherever she wanted. First, she was sent on a campaign to capture Saint-Pierre-le-Moûtier, which she successfully accomplished.

Afterward, Joan's task was to lay siege to La Charité-sur-Loire, but her troops did not have the provisions to follow through. Although the Maid sent letters to various

A view of the towers and walls surrounding La Charité, where Joan attempted a failed siege.

towns to ask for money and supplies, sufficient aid did not materialize from any quarter, and the siege of La Charité ended after a month.

## Bestowing Nobility

Winter had now arrived, making military action more difficult. Charles VII signed a second truce, which would cover the end of 1429 through Easter 1430. In the meantime, the king decided to bestow a gift on the Maid. In December 1429, the king rewarded Joan by raising her family to the status of nobility, signified by a new last name: "du Lys" ("the lily"), the king's royal flower. The grant of nobility included her parents, siblings, and their descendants, both male and female. Joan's brothers began using the surname du Lys but Joan continued to go only by La Pucelle.

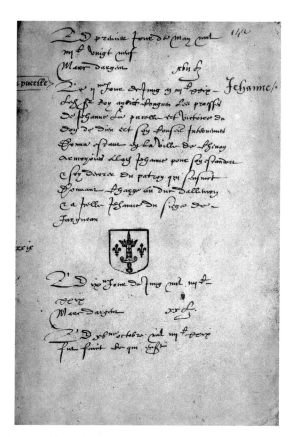

Shown is the original letter from King Charles VII ennobling Joan of Arc and her family.

King Charles VII also granted their family a coat of arms that included the *fleur-de-lys*, as well as a sword holding up a crown. Joan could have used this coat of arms on her banner, but she preferred to use her old standard banner.

The Maid restlessly spent the winter being cared for in royal homes. "They were ready to give her any shining mantle, any beautiful dress, even a title and a noble name," as long as she obeyed the king and his counselors.

# Coat of Arms

During the Middle Ages, soldiers identified friends and foes in battle by their coats of arms. Warriors would wear a garment known as a surcoat decorated with their family design over their armor—thus it was a coat of arms. A family's design was also used as a seal for letters and important documents.

At first, knights chose their own designs, but over time it became something only the king could bestow, and a special organization was designated to keep track of official coats of arms.

Official coats of arms have very specific rules to follow. There were originally only five colors used: bright red, royal blue, emerald green, royal purple, and black. The two metals were gold and silver. The basic rule dictated that metal could be used on color, or color could be used on metal, but metal on metal or color on color was not allowed.

Women were not given coats of arms, so the fact that the king granted one to Joan and her family was exceptional.

The Maid's coat of arms has the inscription *Vive labeur*, which means "Long live labor (work)."

On January 6, Joan turned eighteen years old. In the course of the past year, so much had changed for her. She had left her village an unknown peasant, and now she was a noblewoman, renowned even beyond the borders of her own country, with an entire town of faithful admirers in Orléans and friends in many other locations. On the other hand, the year had also brought her just as many enemies.

## Along the Road to Compiègne

In the spring of 1430, the Maid was staying in the town of Sully, where the king and his court were residing. The latest truce was ending, and Joan had heard that the town of Compiègne was in danger of being attacked by Philip III, the Duke of Burgundy. Word also reached the Maid that the townspeople preferred to die fighting rather than be conquered by the Burgundians. It was that spirit that spurred Joan on to leave the king's court and head for Compiègne to help. However, Joan did not make prior arrangements with the king, neither did she tell him where she was going; she may have even left secretly.

Together with her brothers, her assistant Jean d'Aulon, and a band of two or three hundred volunteers, she headed for Compiègne, first stopping in Melun and then Lagny.

In Melun, the Maid heard from her saints during Easter week (April 22). They told her that she would be captured before Saint John's Day (June 24). "It must be so," they said.

*It was that spirit that spurred Joan on to leave the king's court and head for Compiègne to help.*

"Accept it willingly." Joan begged that when she was taken, she "might die straightway, without long travail in prison." Even though the knowledge of her capture and loss of freedom preyed on the Maid's mind, she did not know where, when, or how it would happen—so she continued on her way as planned.

While Joan was in Lagny, townspeople asked her to come by a statue of the Virgin Mary to pray over a lifeless newborn. The infant had not breathed in three days and was "black as [Joan's]

The Lagny plaque commemorates the miracle of the infant. Joan's prayers brought the baby briefly back to life after he had been dead for three days.

jacket." After the Maid and the townspeople prayed together, the baby yawned three times, and they were able to baptize him properly before he died. The Lagny baby's baptism enabled his family to bury the baby in consecrated ground.

Still on their journey to Compiègne, Joan and her small army fought a band of Anglo-Burgundians of similar size, who were led by a **mercenary** named Franquet d'Arras. The Maid's group won soundly, and d'Arras was taken prisoner. The Armagnacs tried him for robbery, murder, and treachery, and they said he had confessed to all charges. Joan wanted to exchange d'Arras for one of their own, but it happened that the man she wanted to trade him for had already been executed. The judge at d'Arras's trial asked Joan to turn him over for punishment. The Maid replied, "Since that man is dead whom I wanted to have, do with this one what in justice you must do."

At this point, King Charles VII had been disappointed enough by Philip III, Duke of Burgundy, that the king realized that agreements with the duke were not a good idea. The king wrote a letter on May 6 publicly acknowledging that Philip III wanted war rather than peace: "He has, for some time, amused and deceived us by truces and otherwise, under the shadow of good faith." Charles VII's good faith in the Duke of Burgundy had cast a shadow on Joan for almost ten months. Now she was about to fall under a darker shadow.

# CHAPTER 9

# In Her Enemies' Hands

*To save her life, spare neither means nor money
nor any conceivable effort unless you are ready to
face unbelievable disgrace and the reproach of
dire ingratitude.*

—Archbishop Gélu to Charles VII

Around midnight on May 22, 1430, the Maid and several
hundred soldiers left neighboring Crépy to go to the
besieged town of Compiègne. She was warned that she
did not have enough men with her, but she responded, "By
my staff, we are enough! I shall go to see my good friends
in Compiègne."

Joan arrived at dawn on May 23 and her group
successfully slipped into the town. Later that morning, they
heard fighting taking place outside the town. The Maid left
to join the battle, and once she was out there, the enemy
fell back. Joan chased after them, but then it became
apparent that if she and her soldiers continued the chase
and moved farther away from the town, another Anglo-
Burgundian force could get between the Armagnacs and the
town, trapping Joan and her band between them.

Joan and the Armagnacs decided to move back toward
Compiègne. The Maid was farthest from the city because
she had been in the front when chasing the enemy. If she
had wanted to move ahead during the fallback, she could

have, but she preferred to guard her retreating soldiers. It was considered a matter of honor for a captain to be the last one to withdraw.

The people of Compiègne could see the chase that was going on outside the city. The governor of the town, Guillaume de Flavy, ordered that the city gates be closed so the Anglo-Burgundians could not enter. They would have to time the closing of the gates perfectly, so that all the Armagnacs and the Maid could make it inside before the enemy reached the gates. Unfortunately, the plan did not work. Joan, being farthest from the gates, did not make it through before they were shut. The Maid was left outside, surrounded by the enemy with no hope of escape.

*". . . I shall go to see my good friends in Compiègne."*

Since then, historians have tried to determine whether Guillaume de Flavy purposefully betrayed Joan by leaving her outside the gates or if it was an accident. Joan did not blame him. It is hard to say whether he was bribed or not. Some say that Flavy's behavior—aside from this incident—indicates he was a true Armagnac, making an honest mistake seem likely; others think that the city would have been safe with the gates open longer, and he had no excuse for closing them so quickly.

## The Enemy Rejoices

With the enemy swirling around her on horseback, Joan put up a valiant fight. A sour Burgundian archer, determined to stop the young woman who had defeated so many of his fellows, came close enough to grab the Maid by her jacket. He threw her off her horse, onto the ground. The Maid's companions tried vainly to pull her back up on her horse, and a number of them, including

An undated picture depicts the Maid being captured by Burguncians at Compiègne.

her brother Pierre and her assistant, Jean d'Aulon, were taken with her.

The archer who had captured Joan turned her over to his immediate superior, the Bastard of Wandomme, who "more joyful than if he had had a King in his hands, took her hastily to Margny." Philip III was not present at her capture, but "he was very joyous at her taking, for the great renown that she had, for it seemed to many of his side that her works could not but be miraculous." In Margny, Wandomme passed the Maid along to his master, John of Luxembourg. Philip III had the allegiance of John of Luxembourg, so when Luxembourg had to decide between giving Joan back to her own people for a ransom or offering her to the Anglo-Burgundians, the scales were tipped toward the Maid's enemies.

Immediately after they learned of Joan's capture, the faculty at the University of Paris—a major center for religious studies—wrote to Luxembourg to ask that Joan be handed over to them for trial. They complimented him on having taken the Maid prisoner and reminded him that it was his duty as a knight to defend God and the Church. The letter claimed that Joan, whom they called La Pucelle, had offended the honor of God and the Church and wounded the Faith: "For by her means, idolatry, error, false doctrines, and other evils and irreparable hurts have spread throughout the realm." They went on to say that it would be a great evil if he accepted a ransom and returned her to the Armagnacs because she needed to be put on trial to answer the serious charges brought against her.

Another letter followed two weeks later, carried by the Bishop of Beauvais, Pierre Cauchon himself, who was an English sympathizer. The University had offered 6,000 francs (also known as livres) for the Maid, but the English were willing to pay as much as 10,000 francs—the usual ransom set for a king. To them, Joan was literally worth "a king's ransom."

## Joan for Sale

Even with these enormous offers of money, John of Luxembourg was slow to act. His wife and his aunt, who was also Charles VII's godmother, thought highly of the Maid and did not want him to give her to the English. John's wife reportedly threw herself at her husband's feet to beg him not to dishonor himself by selling Joan to her enemies. His aunt had some sway over Luxembourg because he wanted to remain in her will, but once she died on September 18, he no longer had to worry about that inheritance.

From mid-July until John finally sold her in November, Joan was kept in the castle of Beaurevoir. She tried to escape once early on in her captivity, and she tried again from the tower of the Beaurevoir castle in October. She had heard (perhaps from Pierre Cauchon) that all of the people of Compiègne above the age of six were going to be killed. It was a false rumor, but it resulted in Joan despairing over the possible deaths of Compiègne citizens and her being handed over to English soldiers. Joan's saints told her not to try to escape by jumping from the tower in which she was held, but she jumped anyway. The tower was sixty to eighty feet high and the Maid landed on rocky ground. Amazingly, she suffered only a minor head injury and was well again a few days later.

The remains of the castle at Beaurevoir, which was a strong fortress when Joan was imprisoned there during the summer and fall of 1430.

For disobeying her saints, Joan begged her Lord's pardon, which she felt she received. She was also reassured by her saints that Compiègne would be saved by Saint Martin's Day (November 11). John of Luxembourg actually ended the siege on the town at the end of October—happy news indeed for Joan. However, news for the Maid herself was not as good.

A modern photo of the town hall in Compiègne, where a statue of the Maid holding her banner high dominates the square.

The English raised the money to pay for the Maid by taxing the province of Normandy, France. On November 21, 1430, Joan was finally handed over to the English for 10,000 francs, plus an extra 300 for the Bastard of Wandomme for turning Joan over to John of Luxembourg. The English then gave her to the University of Paris so she could be put on trial in a special Catholic court called an Inquisition—whose primary purpose was to oppose and punish heresy (beliefs that were contrary to its religion). This gesture by the English was done with the understanding that if she were found innocent, she would be returned to the English. Basically, Joan was a prisoner of war on loan.

## Irregularities at Joan's Trial

Normally, trials run by the Inquisition followed certain rules. Because Joan's trial was a Church matter, the Maid should have been held in a church prison and guarded by women (nuns). Instead, she was kept in a regular prison where she was guarded by male soldiers.

Also, trials of this nature were supposed to be judged either by the bishop of the accused person's birthplace or in the diocese where the heresy was committed. Pierre Cauchon, bishop of Beauvais, was desperate to be Joan's judge. Because the city of Compiègne fell under the diocese of Beauvais, Cauchon was acceptable as a

A woodcut from Martial d'Auvergne's *Les Vigilles de la Mort du feu Roy Charles VII* (1493) shows Joan being led to prison.

judge, but Beauvais was Armagnac-held and not a safe place to hold the Maid. The University wanted to hold the trial in Paris

# The Inquisition

There were four different Inquisitions in history: the Medieval, the Spanish, the Portuguese, and the Roman, and they took place from the 1100s through the mid-1800s. The Medieval Inquisition was the earliest, and it began with a crusade against a group called the Cathars in particular.

In 1184, Pope Lucius III issued a decree against heretics that said that Cathars and others whose beliefs were outside the church would be despised and expelled, and that the Church's strength would crush them and show that their religion was pure and free from the falsehoods of other beliefs.

When heretics were brought up in the courts, if they did not admit they were wrong and agree to follow Catholic traditions, they were punished. The Church was not allowed to kill anyone, so if they wanted someone put to death, the person would be handed over to the **secular** authorities to execute. Other punishments included having their belongings given to the Church. Through their efforts,

An undated illustration depicts torture devices used during the Spanish Inquisition.

the Church successfully rid themselves of the Cathar movement. Afterward, they continued to hold trials for other suspected heretics and witches, such as Joan.

instead, but it was too close to Charles VII's territory. As a result a decision was made to hold the trial in Rouen, which was safely Burgundian and where nine-year-old King Henry VI was staying. Henry's uncle John, the Duke of Bedford, made arrangements so that the trial could take place at Rouen with their trusted supporter Pierre Cauchon as Joan's judge. However, Rouen was not under Cauchon's diocese, so his participation was an irregular procedure.

## Who Would Help the Maid?

While the English were making elaborate plans for Joan's trial, one wonders what the French and the king were doing to help the imprisoned Maid. It seems that the only effort Charles VII might have made on Joan's behalf was to write a letter to Philip III, insisting that no harm come to the Maid. However, historians are not sure if such a letter was ever written.

England wanted to cast a shadow on Charles VII's claim to the throne by having the young woman who had been so important to his coronation named as a witch. Even if the French king did not feel a personal duty to Joan, it is surprising that he did not make more of an attempt to protect her in his own self-interest.

*. . . one wonders what the French and the king were doing to help the imprisoned Maid.*

In addition to offering a ransom, the king could have made threats toward Anglo-Burgundian prisoners, such as John Talbot who was captured at Patay, if anything happened to Joan. He could have appealed to Pope Martin V (Joan wanted her case to go before the pope). He could have staged an attack where Joan was being held or tried to influence the University of Paris.

With anti-Joan counselors like the Archbishop of Reims—who wrote the people of Reims to tell them that the Maid's capture was her own fault because of her arrogance—and Trémoïlle advising the king, Charles VII might have been discouraged from taking further action on the Maid's behalf. In any case, the king never seemed to need much encouragement to do nothing.

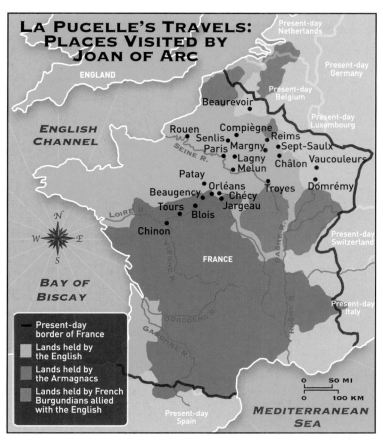

The cities and towns that the Maid journeyed through are traced in this map of France as it was in 1429.

However, Charles VII did receive a letter from his old adviser, Archbishop Jacques Gélu, who said: "To save her life, spare neither means nor money nor any conceivable effort unless you are ready to face unbelievable disgrace and the reproach of dire ingratitude." Although Archbishop Gélu stood nearly alone in this feeling at the time, his assessment was correct—historians have found Charles VII to be shamefully ungrateful. Like many royals, the French king received nicknames: one of his was Charles the Well-Served. He certainly was well-served by the Maid from Domrémy.

The Maid's family felt the horror of her imprisonment deeply. Other friends of Joan did as well. "At Tours the entire population appeared in the streets with bare feet, singing the 'Miserere' [Have Mercy] in penance and affliction. Orléans and Blois made public prayers for her safety." The war captain La Hire, whom Joan had convinced to stop cursing, was reported to have made a couple of unsuccessful attempts to free her, but he was captured during one of them and held for ransom.

The Maid was definitely on her own.

# CHAPTER 10

# The Condemnation

*Here begin the proceedings in matter of faith against a dead woman, Jeanne, commonly known as the Maid.*

—*The Trial Record*

The Maid arrived at her new prison in Rouen on December 23, 1430. She had five guards: three stayed inside her cell and two stayed outside the door. In addition to having no privacy and continually being subject to their taunts and threats, her ankles were shackled with irons chained to her bed. An iron cage was placed in her cell, but that might have been intended to intimidate her because witnesses never saw her in it.

Cauchon actually forbade her to try to escape, threatening that she would be charged with heresy if she attempted it. Joan replied that she had never promised him not to try to escape, so it could not be held against her if she tried. Even though the

This undated artwork captures Joan's fear as she is led into the dark prison.

Maid was young—having just turned nineteen—and emotionally exhausted from being jailed since the previous May, she stood up bravely to powerful, educated men.

The investigators Cauchon had sent to Domrémy to see if they could find any incriminating facts about Joan returned empty-handed. Thus, the trial had to begin without any actual charges filed against the Maid. Charges would have to be made on the basis of the young woman's words alone.

## The Trial Begins

On February 21, 1431, the trial of Jeanne la Pucelle began at eight in the morning in the royal chapel of the Rouen castle. This first examination session commenced with the words, "In the name of the Lord, Amen. Here begin the proceedings in matter of faith against a dead woman, Jeanne, commonly known as the Maid." By *dead*, they meant "dead to the Church," which sounds as though a judgment had been decided against her before the case even started.

Young Joan sat facing dozens of learned men who opposed her and wished nothing more than to see her fail. She was still dressed in her male clothes, which made her appearance rather shocking to those who had never met her. She was also pale and fatigued from her months of imprisonment. The Maid requested that an equal number of clergy from the Armagnac side join them so that both groups could try her, but her plea was rejected.

*Thus, the trial had to begin without any actual charges filed against the Maid.*

The examination began with questions about Joan's name, her background, her childhood, and her faith. It was just the

Joan is chained to the wall in this c. 1880–1900 illustration of her trial interrogation.

first of many interrogations. By March 26, Cauchon and his assistants had interrogated Joan in six public sessions and in nine private ones.

In the second section of the trial, the main prosecutor, Jean d'Estivet, wrote the charges against her. He started out with seventy charges but they were reduced to twelve by the end due to lack of evidence. The second head prosecutor was a monk named Jean Lemaître who represented the Inquisitorial board. Lemaître tended to take a hands-off approach and leave things up to d'Estivet and Cauchon.

*Young Joan sat facing dozens of learned men who . . . wished nothing more than to see her fail.*

Jean d'Estivet was very close to Pierre Cauchon and cut from the same cloth, especially in their loathing of Joan. D'Estivet frequently called Joan names and

In this undated painting, two others are shown in the prison with Joan. The Maid turns to an image of the Virgin Mary for strength while she is imprisoned.

berated her. He also tried to prevent the Maid from praying in the chapel.

Before the trial began, d'Estivet and a man named Nicolas Loiseleur entered the Maid's cell in Rouen, pretending to also be prisoners from her home region in order to win her confidence and get her to incriminate herself. Loiseleur, who introduced himself to Joan as a priest, even listened to her confession (*confession* meaning "the standard Catholic disclosure of everyday sins," not a confession that she had committed heresy). They were unable to uncover anything, but the incident surely showed her the lengths they were willing to go.

The Church's law said that Joan should have a defense counsel (a lawyer representing her). Pierre Cauchon told the Maid that she could choose a counsel from the men in the courtroom, but Joan did not see anyone who would be favorable to her so she turned him down. She would have to deal with the questions and accusations alone.

## Joan Answers Their Questions

Despite the fact that she was uneducated and had no counsel, Joan could easily frustrate her interrogators with her answers. For instance, on February 24, Pierre Cauchon asked her for a second time to promise to answer every question truthfully. She declined because she thought he might ask her about some things—such as her voices—that were personal and none of his business. She said, "It is possible that concerning many things that you may ask me I would not answer the truth . . . for perhaps you might force me to tell something that I have sworn not to tell." She even warned him that he was taking on a "great burden" by being her judge, because she thought he was essentially judging the angels and saints whose orders she had followed.

That same day, the Maid was asked a question that was considered a "trap." The prosecutors asked Joan whether she knew if she was in God's

*. . . Joan could easily frustrate her interrogators with her answers.*

grace. The Church belief was that no one could be sure that he or she was in God's grace; if Joan stated that she knew she was, she would be contradicting the Church's belief, and thus convicting herself of heresy. If she said she knew she was not in

God's grace, she would be admitting she had done something to fall out of grace.

Joan answered, "If I am not, may God place me there; if I am, may God so keep me." She was able to smoothly avoid condemning herself and, according to one of the notaries (officials who wrote down the proceedings of the trial), those present were stupefied by this response.

During the trial, the Maid said there were three things she wished for: her freedom, help for France, and the salvation of her soul. She tried to resign herself that the trial might result in her death, but still she hoped to somehow be delivered from her situation. Joan's voices visited her regularly, providing comfort. They told her to "accept all willingly, heed not your **martyrdom**, you shall come at last into the Kingdom of Paradise." When the saints spoke to her about martyrdom, she was not sure if they were referring to what she had already endured, or what was to come: "I do not know if I shall suffer a greater [martyrdom than imprisonment]; that I leave with our Lord."

*During the trial, the Maid said there were three things she wished for: her freedom, help for France, and the salvation of her soul.*

The questioners wanted to know many details about Joan's saints, including their opinions about the war. "Does God hate the English?" they asked. Her answer: "As to God's love or hate for the English, and what he will do to their souls, I know nothing. But I do know that they will be driven out of France, except those that die here." She was questioned about why her standard (banner) was the only one present in the church when Charles VII was crowned. The Maid replied "It had been present in the perils, and that was reason enough for it to be honored." The prosecutors

## Opposing Points of View

Whether or not clergy members believed Joan heard the voices of saints or devils depended entirely on which side of the war the clergy supported.

In 1429, an Armagnac theological scholar named Jean Gerson authored a defense of the Maid. Gerson wrote a justification for Joan's male clothing, saying that because God chose "our Pucelle" to fight "the enemies of justice" it was up to God to determine what she wore.

Later that year, an anonymous person at the University of Paris wrote a response to Gerson's defense. He complained that the Maid stirred up war, and that she even "got men to kill one another" on a holy day. Anonymous also stated that Joan was working on behalf of the devil: "She was not guided by the Spirit of truth, from which all truth originates, but by the Devil, father of lies, whose plans she endeavours to accomplish."

This argument between Gerson and Anonymous illustrates how the clergy's attitude about Joan's clothing depended not on whether they believed she had a right to wear men's clothes, but whether they agreed with her cause.

wanted to make her banner appear to have magical powers so they could say Joan was a witch and that the devil had helped Charles VII become king.

## Wearing Men's Clothes

Two things that aggravated the prosecutors endlessly were the men's clothes that Joan wore and the belief she held that she knew what God wanted without asking the Church if she was right.

An undated painting of Joan's trial shows her dressed in a man's tunic rather than in a traditional woman's dress.

These problems were actually two sides of the same coin because she said God was the one who told her to don men's clothes while she was accomplishing her mission.

Aside from the Burgundian churchmen finding her male garments to be appalling, they did not like the mission that motivated her to put them on: freeing France from England. The theologians who supported her mission, such as the ones in Poitiers who authorized Charles VII to accept her, approved the garb she wore—for those who agreed with why she wore them could see the usefulness of the clothes. If she had been fighting for the English, her prosecutors would have not thought her clothing heretical at all.

In prison, Joan kept her male clothes, although the prosecutors pushed her to wear women's dress. The Maid did not need men's clothes for ease of travel and fighting anymore, but now the clothes provided her with extra protection from her abusive and aggressive soldier-guards. The Maid had in fact complained to Cauchon and others that her guards had tried to attack her, but her safety was not of vital importance among the prosecutors.

## Joan's Other Crimes

The Maid's confidence in her personal connection with Jesus frustrated her prosecutors, who pressed Joan to agree that they were the authority on what the Lord wanted and that she could not make her own spiritual decisions. She answered that she turned to Jesus, Mary, and the saints for guidance, and "it seems to me that our Lord and the Church are one and the same, and that no one should make difficulties about that."

Joan also asserted that only the Church in Heaven could judge her. "I firmly believe that I have not been faulty in our Christian faith," she stated, still unshakable. However, she was willing, even eager, to have her case brought before the pope, Martin V. Cauchon and the English refused to do that as there was a chance it might lead to her release. The pope actually died while the Maid was on trial, and the new one was not officially notified about her situation.

> "I firmly believe that I have not been faulty in our Christian faith," she stated, still unshakable.

The list of charges against Joan was completed on April 5 and sent to the University of Paris and King of England for

Joan told her prosecutors she looked to Christ, the Madonna, and her saints for guidance. In this undated painting of the Maid, the Madonna and child, and Archangel Michael, Joan is shown holding the scales of judgment.

comments. The twelve "articles of accusation" were lengthy, but a summarized version explains that Joan's guilt lay in, "1) the revelations and apparitions of angels and saints; 2) a miraculous 'sign' that Joan had given to the dauphin Charles that she was sent by God; 3) her confidence in the advice and teachings of her angels and saints; 4) her predictions of future events; 5) her men's dress; 6) her tactics in war; 7) the treatment of her parents in leaving home without their knowledge; 8) the act of leaping from the tower in Compiègne; 9) her assurance that she would go to heaven; 10) her assertion that God is on the side of the French and not the English; 11) her vow of [purity] to her angels and saints without counsel of a priest; and 12) her unwillingness to obey the Church on earth."

In other words, if she had been on their side, nothing she had done would have been a crime. Because she was on the opposing side, however, even leaving her parents' house was considered a crime worth punishing.

Cauchon and his men had decided what Joan was guilty of. Now, all that was left was to force the Maid to admit her crimes.

# CHAPTER 11

# The Maid's Final Days

*I would rather be beheaded seven times than suffer burning.*

On April 16, 1431, Joan grew ill after eating a fish sent to her by Pierre Cauchon. It is uncertain if the fish was poisoned, bad, or merely too rich for the Maid, who was used to eating very simply, but she grew very ill with vomiting and fever. D'Estivet said that the illness was Joan's own fault and yelled at her with the doctor present. His treatment of the Maid bothered the court recorders (notaries), one of whom said later that D'Estivet got what he deserved when he was found floating in a Rouen sewer in 1438.

It seemed as though Joan might not survive, but she improved enough for them to start the next phase of her Inquisition—the Admonitions. Although the Admonitions were defined as "warnings," the goal during this phase was not just to warn the person, but to force him or her to confess or repent—meaning to apologize and promise to sin no more. Torture was also allowed during this stage of the trial.

## The Threat of Torture

Joan was threatened with torture on May 9. She was brought to the Great Tower of Rouen, where she could see the implements of torture for herself. When the prosecutors questioned her on issues they had already interrogated her

# The Inquisition Torture Practices

During the Middle Ages, the Inquisition (the court system of the Catholic church) approved the use of torture to obtain confessions from people accused of crimes. However, the church was supposed to follow certain rules about torture: no bloodshed, mutilation, or death. Sometimes, it broke the rules. It could also turn to the secular courts, which did not have such rules to follow and were allowed to execute criminals.

Inquisitors had devices devoted to causing pain, such as the rack (which pulled joints out of their sockets) and the thumbscrew (which crushed fingers and toes). One can only wonder what devices were shown to Joan to encourage her to confess.

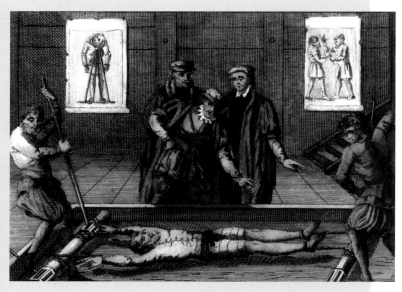

A sixteenth-century copper engraving portraying the torture of the rack.

about, she said, "Truly, if you were to have me torn limb from limb and send my soul out of my body, I would say nothing else. And if I did say anything, afterwards I should always say that you had made me say it by force." She spoke boldly, but even she had a breaking point.

Pierre Cauchon gathered a council of twelve men and asked them if they thought Joan should be tortured. When only three agreed that she should (one of whom was Nicolas Loiseleur, friend of d'Estivet), Cauchon did not pursue it, but the English nobles were growing restless. The University of Paris had been working on this case since January, and what did it have? It had listed twelve articles (charges) that it believed Joan was guilty of, and the king of England agreed with its conclusions, but there was still no confession.

## Obtaining a Confession

In order to frighten the Maid into an admission of guilt, on May 24, Joan was brought to a cemetery. There, University of Paris theologian Guillaume Erard gave a long sermon about her evil ways to a crowd that included English noblemen and their supporters, as well as commoners. Erard stated that Charles VII was as guilty as Joan because he had allowed her to support him. Then the Maid was told to sign an admission of her guilt or burn at the stake.

The executioner was present, so Joan must have thought the court meant to kill her on the spot if she did not confess. The court encouraged her repeatedly to sign and told her that signing would mean she would not have to return to the Rouen prison. "I would rather sign it than burn," the Maid said, surrendering. By signing the document—called her recantation—she was admitting her guilt and renouncing her previous behavior.

However, a mysterious aspect of her recantation was that the document Joan signed was much shorter, according to witnesses, than the one that was submitted to the court. The witnesses believed that the documents were *switched*, which meant that the Maid had agreed to plead guilty to a short number of crimes, but the prosecutors claimed she confessed to a longer list.

Another interesting point about her recantation was that Joan was asked by her prosecutors to sign the confession with a cross next to her name. This was an ironic request because previously, Joan had put a cross on letters that she sent as decoys—ones that she meant to confuse the enemy if the letters were taken from her messenger. The cross was intended to alert the recipient that the letter was not to be believed. It must have amused the Maid that the English had asked her to mark her confession as false. In fact, the Maid was said to have smiled or laughed at one point during the proceedings, and perhaps it was at the moment when she added her cross.

*Then the Maid was told to sign an admission of her guilt or burn at the stake.*

After she signed her recantation, Joan asked, "Now, you churchmen, take me to your prison, and let me be no longer in the hands of the English." Unfortunately, that request turned out to be overly optimistic because Cauchon commanded, "Take her to where you found her." Despite the fact that Joan was expecting that her life would be different now, the only thing that changed was that she had on women's clothes in the same location with the same guards. She was more vulnerable than ever.

## Revoking the Recantation

The Maid continued to be chained to her bed in a secure location, sentenced to "perpetual imprisonment, with the bread of sorrow and the water of affliction, that you may weep for your sins, and nevermore commit them." A few days later, Joan began committing a crime punishable by death—she began wearing men's clothes again. Some accounts state that she did it because her guards took her female attire and only left her male garments. Others say that the Maid put the men's clothing on because she needed the protection, due to increased attempts of assault once she had recanted. In any case, Cauchon appeared on May 27 to see if it was true that Joan was once again wearing men's clothes.

During this visit, the Maid was ready to reject her recantation. She told Cauchon and his companions that she had heard from her saints, who told her that she should have replied boldly to Erard at the cemetery. "If I said that God had not sent me, I should damn myself; it is true that God sent me. My voices have since told me that I did a great injury in confessing that I had not done well in what I had done. All that I said and revoked that Thursday, I did only because of fear of the fire." Defiant, but still making an attempt at being cooperative, Joan said "If the judges wish it I will resume women's clothes; for the rest, I will do nothing about it."

The fact of the matter was that Cauchon and his men did not want her to wear women's clothing now. They might have even arranged the attacks on her person or the disappearance of her women's attire. If they could find she was wearing men's clothes, she could be proclaimed a relapsed heretic (one who had returned to heretical ways) and that would pave the way for her death sentence.

When the clerk was writing Joan's responses to Cauchon's questions, he noted in the margin that she had made a "responsio mortifera,"—meaning a "mortal answer" that would now seal her fate. And so, she was proclaimed a relapsed heretic. The Maid reproached the churchmen as they left her. She felt that if she had been kept in a church prison where she could be guarded by women, she would not have had to put on the men's clothes again.

In this page of the 1431 trial transcript, dated May 23, Joan says that even "if I were at the place of execution, and I saw the fire lighted . . . I would maintain what I have said at this trial until death."

Cauchon told the Englishmen who were waiting outside, "Farewell, it is done." He had done his part to assure that Joan would not survive the outcome of the trial

## To the Fire

At eight o'clock in the morning on Wednesday, May 30, 1431, nineteen-year-old Joan of Domrémy was led into Rouen's Old Market Place where a crowd of Englishmen, church members, and townspeople were gathered. At times during her imprisonment, the Maid had hoped to be rescued, but she had no such hope now. "Alas!" she lamented, "I would rather be beheaded seven times than suffer burning."

*We throw you out of the unity of the Church, we discard you as a rotten member.*

She heard herself pronounced a relapsed heretic who had profaned the holy name of God. Her prosecutors declared her worthless and wicked, and said, "We throw you out of the unity of the Church, we discard you as a rotten member."

Cauchon and the Englishmen were both in a great hurry to have the Maid executed, perhaps for fear that she might be able to do some sort of magic to stay alive. However, even though she had already been **excommunicated** and was officially no longer a member of the church, they allowed her to have **communion**.

Joan still blamed Cauchon for needing to wear men's clothes for her own safety and her subsequent **condemnation** as a relapsed heretic. She told him, "Bishop, I die through you!"

The Maid asked for a cross, and she was given a little wooden cross by an unknown Englishman who made it out of an end of a

The Maid is being led to her execution in this 1867 painting by Isidore Patrois.

stick. She placed it inside her dress. There was a church nearby, so Joan asked the monks attending her to bring a cross from the church so it could be the last thing she saw: "I would have the cross on which God hung be ever before my eyes while life lasts in me." This request was carried out.

"Jesus!" was the last word spoken by Joan of Arc, which she uttered several times before she died.

Although no one had attempted to stop the execution, many witnesses were shaken by it. An Englishman told one of the monks present that, "he had seen a white dove flying from the direction of France at the moment when she was giving up the ghost" and he believed he had killed a saint. The official executioner also said that he "greatly feared to be damned" for what he had done, and Jean Alespée, priest of the Rouen church, wept, "I wish that my soul were where I believe the soul of this girl is."

# After the Maid's Death

To confirm that Joan was really dead, the Maid's body was shown to the public before it was burned again to turn her to ashes. Afterward, the executioner told at least two people that Joan's heart had not burned. Her ashes were scattered in the Seine River to prevent them from being saved as holy relics—objects that belonged to or were touched by Jesus or a saint were thought to sometimes produce miracles.

Joan's father, Jacques, died that same year, reportedly from grief over his daughter.

This c. 1851 print shows a dove flying overhead as Joan of Arc is burned at the stake.

# Joan of Arc Relics

In 1867, a human bone, a cat bone, a piece of cloth, and chunks of wood were discovered in a Paris attic inside a jar that was labeled, "Remains found under the stake of Joan of Arc, virgin of Orléans." The relics were believed to be authentic, even by the Vatican, and were kept at a church in Chinon for years. The cat bone seemed authentic due to the medieval custom of burning black cats with witches (even though the Maid was not technically accused of being a witch).

Finally a forensic science team studied the relics in 2007 and found out what they really were—remains from an Egyptian mummy!

This photograph shows the remains that were believed to belong to Joan of Arc. Eventually, they were proved to be much older.

# CHAPTER 12

# Saint Joan of Arc

*May it now and henceforward venerate her as a most brilliantly shining light of the Church Triumphant.*

— From the Canonization Pronouncement for Saint Joan of Arc

The Anglo-Burgundian faction had hoped that Joan's death would cast Charles VII as a pretender to the throne who was aided by a heretic. However, the Maid's successes in 1429 marked the turning point in the Hundred Years' War from which England was never able to recover.

Two years after Joan's death, Arthur de Richemont, who had fought alongside the Maid at the Battle of Patay, returned to Charles VII's court. His return was enabled by the exit of Joan's old foe Georges de la Trémoïlle. Trémoïlle had become so unpopular at court before he left that an attempt was made on his life by young men who supported the queen and her mother. Apparently, Trémoïlle's rotund body kept a knife wound from being fatal, but the incident encouraged him to move elsewhere. Richemont's return to favor gave him a chance to work harder to expel the English army from France.

In the fall of 1435, England's John, Duke of Bedford, died in the castle in Rouen where Joan had been imprisoned four years earlier. At about the same time, France's Philip III,

Duke of Burgundy, changed sides. Once Burgundy had joined Charles VII, the Anglo-Burgundian alliance was over, and England was fighting a united France. The following year, the French army captured Paris.

## Of Plays and Imposters

That same year, an unknown playwright authored *The Mystery of the Siege of Orléans*, a huge production featuring more than a hundred characters, including Jehanne la Pucelle, of course, and twenty different settings. This play was commissioned by French nobleman Gilles de Rais who had fought at the siege of Orléans and gave himself an impressive role in the play.

Between 1436 and 1440, an impostor tried to pass herself off as the Maid. Because Joan was still on people's minds and there were no pictures of her, it was not entirely surprising that an impersonator would try to convince the public that she was really the Maid. What is surprising is that Joan's brothers went along with the pretense, which was essentially just a moneymaking scheme. The fake Joan's behavior did not echo the real Maid at all, and she did not have an impact on France's political affairs.

Gilles de Rais, a nobleman and soldier who commissioned a play about the siege of Orléans.

# Gilles de Rais (1404–1440)

Gilles de Rais was a French noble who enjoyed warfare. He fought in some of Joan's campaigns and was present at the coronation of Charles VII. In 1435, he retired from military action and became involved with theatrical productions, such as *The Mystery of the Siege of Orléans*.

He spent his family's fortune and secretly became a serial killer, committing horrible crimes against children. In 1440, he was put on trial for his crimes and executed. Although it was generally believed that he was indeed guilty, the trial was not a fair one as he was tortured to confess and had no witnesses for the defense. In later years, a fairytale about a serial killer named "Bluebeard" was supposedly based on him.

Gilles de Rais was thought to be the inspiration for the chilling Bluebeard character. Shown is an engraving of Bluebeard and his wife from Charles Perrault's *Fairytales*.

## Clearing Joan's Name

In 1449, two important events took place: Charles VII initiated a campaign to take back the region of Normandy, and supporters of Joan of Arc began asking for an examination of her trial. Normandy was won in April 1450 and Aquitaine secured in 1453; the Hundred Years' War was over. The English continued to hold the port city of Calais, but the rest of the country was French once more.

The capture of Normandy was an important step in conducting an investigation of Joan's trial. Until that time no one could see the trial records in Rouen because the town was under English control. Once Rouen was conquered, Charles VII appointed clergyman Guillaume Bouillé to look into the matter, stating that because the English military had seized Joan the Maid and "by means of this trial and the great hatred that our enemies

This illustration from Jean de Wavrin's fifteenth-century *Chroniques de l'Angleterre* shows Normandy soldiers at war. British rule in Normandy ended in 1450.

An undated portrait of Pope Calixtus III, who oversaw Joan's nullification trial, is shown here.

have against her, they caused her death [unjustly] and against reason, very cruelly indeed; for this reason we wish to know the truth of the aforesaid trial."

Bouillé quickly gathered testimony from seven people associated with the trial, and he concluded that Joan's only crime was that she aided Charles VII—not that she was a heretic. Because she had been found guilty of being a heretic through a Church trial, however, it was up to the Church to nullify (cancel) the verdict. In 1455, Isabelle Romée (Joan's mother) and Joan's brothers, Pierre and Jean, sent Pope Calixtus III a petition asking that the condemnation trial verdict be thrown out and the Maid's good name restored. The pope agreed to assign Jean Bréhal, the Inquisitor-General of France, to Joan's case.

## The Nullification Trial

The **nullification** trial (also known as the rehabilitation trial) officially opened on November 7, 1455 with a statement from Isabelle Romée: "What has long been hidden may be clearly revealed and become public, that is to say that this trial was marred by fraud, by violence and equally by iniquity [injustice]." From November through the summer of the following year, investigators gathered information about Joan and her life by traveling to the various towns where she had been and interviewing people who knew her.

The testimonies Bréhal gathered about the Maid showed a young woman who was devoted to her religion, to her mission, and to her people. Bréhal concluded that Joan's visions were real and that sometimes God preferred to choose a servant among the humble and weak as a way to show His strength.

By the time the trial started, Pierre Cauchon, the Bishop of Beauvais had already died. Following Joan's execution, he had become the Bishop of Lisieux in Normandy and continued to work for the English government until his death in 1442 of heart failure. Cauchon's relatives were asked to speak for him at the nullification trial, but they declined and instead chose to send a statement blaming Joan's fate on the English faction and its hatred of the Maid.

*The testimonies . . . showed a young woman who was devoted to her religion, to her mission, and to her people.*

The study of the trial showed irregularities in the way it was held: the location of the trial, that Joan was not in a church prison, that she did not have a defense counsel, that there were no eyewitnesses besides the defendant, that the prosecution openly hated the defendant, and that no evidence favorable to the accused was offered. Clearing Joan's name was a straightforward case.

In Rouen on July 7, 1456, the Church nullified the condemnation trial in a special ceremony: "We proclaim that Joan did not contract any taint of infamy and that she shall be and is washed clean of such." This ceremony was repeated in towns across France, including Orléans, where Isabelle Romée had been living since 1440. Consequently, Joan was deemed a martyr (someone who chooses death rather than renouncing his or her faith) rather than a heretic.

## On Becoming a Saint

Over the centuries, no group of people have loved the Maid more than the citizens of Orléans, so it is only fitting that it would be a Bishop of Orléans, Félix Dupanloup, who would initiate proceedings to make Joan a saint. He petitioned the pope in 1869, asking that the Maid be canonized, or declared a saint.

In 1894, she was named "Venerable" (the first step in becoming a saint) and in 1901, Joan was beatified. Beatification, the step before canonization, grants that the candidate is a martyr or has done miracles, and he or she is "blessed" and may be venerated (honored) in a limited way.

Then Joan had just one more trial. Her canonization trial took place from 1914 to 1919, and she was finally declared a saint on May 16, 1920, in Saint Peter's Basilica at the Vatican in Rome. The decree read: "May the whole Catholic world hear, and just as it has

Félix Dupanloup of Orléans was the bishop who initiated the proceedings to declare the Maid a saint.

come to admire her brave deeds in defense of her country, may it now and henceforward venerate her as a most brilliantly shining light of the Church Triumphant."

# Catholic Saints

In modern times, it is much more common for someone to be declared a saint than it was in the past centuries. It is believed that Pope John Paul II, who was the pope from 1978 to 2005, canonized as many or more saints than *all* of the previous popes combined. Pope John Paul II streamlined the procedure for canonization in 1983, which made it a quicker process. Even so, there is traditionally a five-year wait after a person's death before the process of becoming a saint can begin. Many people wanted to start the procedure immediately after the death of Mother Teresa of Calcutta in 1997, and the pope did decide to waive the five-year waiting period after only two years. In 2003, Mother Teresa was beatified after a miracle that occurred the previous year was attributed to her. In order to achieve canonization, she must be recognized as bringing about another miracle.

Mother Teresa of Calcutta was beatified in 2003.

The first saint born in the United States was Elizabeth Ann Seton (1774–1821). She founded a free school for Catholic children in Maryland and the American Sisters of Charity, a religious community for women. The second American saint was Katharine Drexel (1858–1955), who spent a substantial inheritance establishing the Sisters of the Blessed Sacrament—an order that started dozens of Native American schools and missions and more than a hundred schools for African Americans, including Xavier University.

An oil painting c. 1804 of American saint Elizabeth Ann Seton.

# Joan of the Arts

In 1894, Emile Huet created a list of more than four hundred plays and musical compositions about Joan of Arc. That was twenty-six years before she was named a saint, and she had already motivated hundreds of playwrights and musicians to immortalize her in their creations. So many works of art have been inspired by the Maid that there is no complete list of them anywhere.

Not all of the works about Joan have portrayed her positively, though. Shakespeare's 1590 portrayal of the Maid in *Henry VI* reflects the English bias of the day by making her a villainous witch who is legitimately executed. When George Bernard Shaw wrote his play, *Saint Joan*, he tried to make the trial seem fairly run and both sides sympathetic. Shaw was very fond of Joan, though, and when he died, his ashes were scattered around a statue of the Maid in his garden.

Mark Twain, popular author of *The Adventures of Huckleberry Finn* and *The Adventures of Tom Sawyer*, spent twelve years researching the Maid so he could write *Personal Recollections of Joan of Arc*. He published it under the name Louis de Conte rather than his own because he wanted people to take it seriously. Twain said of his book: "Possibly the book may not sell, but that is nothing—it was written for love."

This poster advertises the critically acclaimed silent movie *The Passion of Joan of Arc*.

In 1928, Danish filmmaker Carl Dreyer directed *The Passion of Joan of Arc*, a silent film widely considered to be one of the best movies of all time. Maria Falconetti, the actress who starred as Joan, found the experience so draining that she never acted again.

## From Politics to Fashion

In addition to books, plays, and movies about Joan, she has also inspired operas, paintings, statues, and political discourse. During World War I, the United States used an illustration of Joan to encourage women to buy war savings stamps. The copy read "Joan of Arc saved France; Women of America Save Your Country." She was also pictured on posters during World War II, including an anti-English one that showed British warplanes flying above Joan at the stake, and the copy reading, "They Always Return to the Scene of Their Crimes!"

Even today, French politicians speak of Joan as being on their side. In 2007, however, future French president Nicolas Sarkozy spoke out against citing the Maid this way, declaring, "Joan rises above all the parties, and no one can hijack her. Joan is France!"

That sentiment is shared by many in France, and is evident in their annual Joan of Arc celebrations. In June, Reims holds a two-day *Fetes Johanniques* that features a procession of 2,000 actors, including ones representing Charles VII and the Maid herself.

A War Savings Stamps poster from World War I urges women to save their country the way Joan of Arc saved France.

Joan of Arc holds different meanings for those she influences. In the twenty-first century, many new depictions of Joan have sprouted, including characters in numerous computer games and television shows and even by fashion designers who have taken her as their inspiration. The world is not done with the Maid yet.

French author André Malraux captured the essence of the Maid's legacy on a plaque at the site of her death. It reads (in translation), "Joan of Arc, without tomb and without portrait, you who knew that the grave of heroes is the heart of the living."

Saint Joan's courage, dedication, eloquence, and intense desire to do what was right make her an appealing hero and enduring inspiration.

A statue of Saint Joan in the Cathedral Church of Saint John the Divine in New York City captures the Maid's holiness.

# Glossary

**Anglo-Burgundians**—a group of combined English soldiers and their Burgundian supporters.

**anointed**—when oil is put on a person during a religious ceremony as a sign of holy purpose.

**chivalry**—the medieval principles governing knighthood and knightly conduct; honorable behavior.

**communion**—a sacred ceremony in which bread and wine are blessed, eaten, and drunk in remembrance of Jesus's death.

**condemnation**—an expression of strong disapproval; pronouncing as wrong; a final judgment of guilty in a criminal case and the punishment that is imposed.

**constable**—in the Middle Ages, the constable of France was the lieutenant-general of the king and outranked all the nobles.

**devotee**—a strongly enthusiastic follower.

**ecclesiastical**—of or relating to a church or to an established religion.

**excommunicated**—to be deprived of the right of church membership.

**exorcised**—to have evil spirits cast out of a person by prayers or incantations.

**Feast of the Ascension Day**—a celebration of Jesus Christ's ascension to heaven forty days after his resurrection.

**friar**—a member of a religious order who is called to a life of poverty in service to a community.

**Lent**—a period of spiritual preparation for Easter, which begins on Ash Wednesday and lasts forty days (excluding Sundays), ending on Easter.

**longbow**—a long, hand-drawn bow, such as that used in medieval England, which sometimes exceeded six feet in length.

**martyrs**—people who are put to death or endure great suffering on behalf of a belief, principle, or cause.

**martyrdom**—the condition, sufferings, or death of a martyr.

**Mass**—the religious service at which the sacrament of the Eucharist, or Communion, is performed.

**mercenary**—a person hired to fight for a country other than his or her own.

**nullification**—the process of declaring something legally invalid.

**piety**—religious devotion and reverence to God.

**pious**—having or exhibiting religious reverence; earnestly compliant in the observance of religion; devout.

**prophecy**—knowledge of the future usually said to be obtained from a heavenly source.

**secular**—not specifically relating to religion or to a religious body. The secular court system was not run by the Catholic Church.

**siege**—the surrounding and blockading of a city, town, or fortress by an army attempting to capture it.

**squire**—a young nobleman attendant for a knight in feudal hierarchy.

# Bibliography

**Books**

Attwater, Donald with Catherine Rachel John. *Penguin Dictionary of Saints*. New York: Penguin, 1995.

Barrett, W. P. *The Trial of Jeanne D'Arc*, Translated into English from the Original Latin and French Documents. New York: Gotham House, Inc., 1932.

Colby, Charles W., ed., *Selections from the Sources of English History, B.C. 55–A.D. 1832*. London: Longmans, Green, 1920.

Denis, Léon. *The Mystery of Joan of Arc*. Arthur Conan Doyle, translator. New York: E.P. Dutton and Co., 1925.

DeVries, Kelly. *Joan of Arc: A Military Leader*. Gloucestershire: Sutton Publishing, 1999.

d'Orliac, Jehanne. *Yolande d'Anjou, la reine des quatre royaumes*. Paris: Plon, 1933.

France, Anatole. *La Vie de Jeanne d'Arc (The Life of Joan of Arc)*, vol. 1 and 2. Translated by Winifred Stephens. New York: 1908.

Gordon, Mary. *Joan of Arc*. London: Weidenfeld & Nicolson, 2000.

Gower, Ronald Sutherland. *Joan of Arc*. London: John C. Nimmo, 1893.

Guizot, Francois Pierre Guillaume, Translated by Robert Black. *A Popular History of France From The Earliest Times, Volume III of VI*.

*Internet Medieval Source Book* translated by Belle Tuten from M. Vallet de Vireville, ed. *Chronique de la Pucelle ou Chronique de Cousinot*, 1859.

Kennedy, Angus J. and Kenneth Varty, ed. *Ditie de Jehanne D'Arc by Christine de Pisan*. Oxford: Society for the Study of Mediæval Languages and Literature, 1977.

Michelet, Jules. *Joan of Arc*. Ann Arbor, MI: University of Michigan Press, 1967.

Murray, T. Douglas, ed. *Jeanne D'Arc: Maid of Orleans Deliverer of France, Being the Story of her Life, her Achievements, and her Death, as attested on Oath and set forth in the Original Documents*. London: William Heinemann, 1903.

Oliphant, Margaret. *Jeanne d'Arc*. New York: G.P. Putnam's Sons/The Knickerbocker Press, 1896.

Pernoud, Regine. *Joan of Arc: By Herself and Her Witnesses*. Lanham, MD: Scarborough House, 1969.

Pernoud, Regine and Marie-Veronique Clin, translated and revised by Jeremy duQuesnay Adams. *Joan of Arc: Her Story*. New York: St. Martin's, 1999.

Quicherat, Jules-Étienne-Joseph, ed. *Procès de condamnation et de réhabilitation de Jeanne d'Arc, dite la Pucelle* (Condemnation and Rehabilitation Trials of Joan of Arc). 5 vols. Paris: Jules Renouard, 1841–1849; reprinted, New York: Johnson, 1965.

Ramsay, James H. *The Scholar's History of England*. London: H. Milford Oxford University Press, 1892.

Rankin, Daniel and Claire Quintal, translators. *The First Biography of Joan of Arc with the Chronicle Record of a Contemporary Account by Anonymous*. University of Pittsburg Press, 1964.

Sackville-West, Vita. *Saint Joan of Arc.* New York City: Grove Press, 2001.

Taylor, Craig. *Joan of Arc: La Pucelle.* Manchester, UK: Manchester University Press, 2006.

Trask, Willard. *Joan of Arc: In Her Own Words.* New York: Books & Co, A Turtle Point Imprint, 1996.

Twain, Mark. *Personal Recollections of Joan of Arc.* San Francisco, CA: Ignatius Press, 1989.

Warner, Marina. *Joan of Arc: the Image of Female Heroism.* Berkeley, CA: University of California Press, 1981.

**Web Sites**

Coffin, Haskell. *Joan of Arc Saved France—Women of America, Save Your Country—Buy War Savings Stamps.* New York: The United States Printing & Lithograph Co., 1918. From the Louisiana State Archives. http://louisdl.louislibraries.org/u?/AAW,19 (accessed July 9, 2008).

*Official Pronouncement of Canonization of Saint Joan of Arc,* maidofheaven.com.

Pinzino, Jane Marie. *"The Condemnation and Rehabilitation Trials of Joan of Arc."* International Joan of Arc Society site, hosted by Southern Methodist University. http://www.smu.edu/ijas/pinzino.html

**Articles**

Crawford, Amy. "France's Leading Lady." *Smithsonian Magazine,* June 1, 2007.

# Source Notes

The following list identifies the sources of the quoted material found in this book. The first and last few words of each quotation are cited, followed by the source. Complete information on each source can be found in the Bibliography.

**Abbreviations:**

**CRT**—*The Condemnation and Rehabilitation Trials of Joan of Arc*
**DJA**—*Ditie de Jehanne D'Arc*
**FLL**—*France's Leading Lady*
**JA**—*Joan of Arc (Michelet)*
**JAG**—*Joan of Arc (Gower)*
**JD'A**—*Jeanne d'Arc*
**JD'AMO**—*Jeanne d'Arc, Maid of Orleans*
**JAMF**—*Joan of Arc: Maid of France.*
**JAHW**—*Joan of Arc: By Herself and Her Witnesses*
**JAHS**—*Joan of Arc: Her Story*
**JALP**—*Joan of Arc: La Pucelle*
**JAOW**—*Joan of Arc: In Her Own Words*
**JAIFH**—*Joan of Arc: the Image of Female Heroism*
**JASF**—*Joan of Arc Saved France—Women of America, Save Your Country*
**LSA**—*Louisiana State Archives*
**MJA**—*The Mystery of Joan of Arc*
**PH**—*A Popular History of France*
**PR**—*Personal Recollections of Joan of Arc*
**SSEH**—*Selections from the Sources of English History*
**SJA**—*Saint Joan of Arc*

**TFBJA**—*The First Biography of Joan of Arc*
**TJA**—*The Trial of Joan of Arc*
**VJD**—*La Vie de Jeanne d'Arc*
**YD**—*Yolande d'Anjou, la reine des quatre royaumes*

## INTRODUCTION: Defender of France
PAGE 1 *"I must go . . . have it so."*: JAOW, p. 16
PAGE 1 *"You must . . . of France,"*: JAOW, p. 7
PAGE 1 *"I am a . . . and warfare."*: JAOW, p. 7

## CHAPTER 1: Childhood in a Land at War
PAGE 2 *"Although France . . . should save it."*: JAG
PAGE 2 *"Like heralds . . . new joy,"*: JAHS, p. 55
PAGE 2 *"In my country . . . when I [left],"*: JAHS, p. 220
PAGE 4 *"Because the people . . . and fervor."*: JD'AMO, Romée testimony
PAGE 10 *"We have not . . . English like you."*: YD, p. 56

## CHAPTER 2: Sacred Voices
PAGE 11 *"Since God . . . would have gone."*: JAOW, p. 11
PAGE 12 *"Who did not . . . Middle Ages?"*: JA, p. 4
PAGE 12 *"had had many . . . beautiful revelations."*: JAHW, p. 46
PAGES 13–14 *"They spoke . . . sweet and soft,"*: JAOW, p. 7
PAGE 14 *"about the . . . of France,"*: JAOW, p. 6
PAGE 14 *"since God . . . would have gone."*: JAOW, p. 11
PAGE 16 *"that she would . . . to his coronation."*: JD'AMO, Poulengey testimony
PAGE 16 *"take her back . . . box her ears."*: JD'AMO, Laxart testimony

## CHAPTER 3: A Peasant Girl Leads the Way
PAGE 18 *"Surrender to the Maid . . . in France."*: JAIFH, p. 58
PAGE 18 *"I must be with . . . will have it so."*: JAOW, p. 16
PAGE 19 *"Her words . . . believe, divine."*: JAHS, p. 87
PAGE 21 *"Go, go . . . come of it."*: SSEH, p. 115
PAGES 21–22 *"ready to do . . . to see him.]"*: JAHW, p. 39
PAGE 24 *"beautiful and shapely."*: JALP, p. 347
PAGE 24 *"entirely divine."*: JALP, p. 93
PAGE 25 *"Most noble dauphin . . . in France."*: JAOW, p. 164
PAGE 27 *"Render to the Maid . . . very great injury."*: JAHW, pp. 70–71
PAGE 29 *"I loved [my] sword . . . I kill any."*: JAOW, p. 27

## CHAPTER 4: Lifting the Siege
PAGE 30 *"All is yours; enter!"*: JAME, Vol. 1, p. 173
PAGE 31 *"When I saw her . . . my swearing."*: JAHW, p. 63
PAGE 31 *"in the matter . . . preparing the artillery."*: JAHW, p. 63
PAGE 31 *"She behaved as if . . . [the art of] war."*: JD'AMO, d'Armagnac testimony
PAGE 31 *"never allowed . . . was stolen."*: JALP, p. 302
PAGE 32 *"right joyful at her coming."*: JAHW, p. 83
PAGE 32 *"The counsel of the Lord . . . King of Heaven."*: JAHW, pp. 81–82
PAGE 32 *"where she was greatly wished for."*: JAHW, p. 82
PAGE 33 *"felt already comforted . . . on which she rode."*: JAHS, p. 41
PAGE 34 *"the blood . . . was spilling!"*: JAHW, p. 86
PAGE 34 *"so soon as you . . . have your head."*: JAHS, p. 43
PAGE 34 *"of this . . . let her know."*: JAHS, p. 43
PAGE 35 *"Jhesus Maria, Jehanne La Pucelle,"*: JD'AMO, Pasquerel testimony
PAGE 35 *"I would have sent you . . . not killed there."*: JD'AMO, Pasquerel testimony

# Image Credits

## About the Author

**Tabatha Yeatts** imagines life during the Hundred Years' War from the comforts of her Maryland home, which she shares with three kids, two cats, one husband, one dog, and one bird. In addition to newspaper and magazine articles, short stories, and poems, she has written books about Albert Einstein, forensic pioneers, the Holocaust, and Mae West. She wishes she could have watched Joan of Arc in action, but is glad the Maid never met Mae West.

# Index